W9-BLR-116

A/B

TESTING

A/B
TESTING

THE MOST POWERFUL WAY TO TURN CLICKS INTO CUSTOMERS

DAN SIROKER   PETE KOOMEN

WITH CARA HARSHMAN

WILEY

Cover design: Ryan Myers

Published by John Wiley & Sons, Inc., Hoboken, New Jersey.

Published simultaneously in Canada.

For general information about our other products and services, please contact our Customer Care Department within the United States at (800) 762–2974, outside the United States at (317) 572–3993 or fax (317) 572–4002.

Wiley publishes in a variety of print and electronic formats and by print-on-demand. Some material included with standard print versions of this book may not be included in e-books or in print-on-demand. If this book refers to media such as a CD or DVD that is not included in the version you purchased, you may download this material at http://booksupport.wiley.com. For more information about Wiley products, visit www.wiley.com.

Library of Congress Cataloging-in-Publication Data:
Siroker, Dan.
   A/B testing : the most powerful way to turn clicks into customers / Dan Siroker, Pete Koomen.
     pages cm
     Includes index.
   ISBN 978-1-118-53609-4 (cloth); 978-1-118-65917-5 (ebk); ISBN 978-1-118-65920-5 (ebk)
   1. Organizational effectiveness. 2. Multimedia systems–Social aspects.
3. Application software–Testing.   I. Koomen, Pete, 1982- II. Title.
   HD58.9.S5447 2013
   658.8'3402854678–dc23

                                                                2013016038

Printed in the United States of America

10 9 8 7 6 5 4 3 2 1

Contents

How A/B Testing Helped Win the White House—Twice

The $57 Million Button

It was 2007 when then-Senator Barack Obama was running for President, and no one but the *Des Moines Register* seemed to think he had a chance of winning the Democratic primary.

DAN: I was a product manager at Google at the time, and I'd seen Obama speak at our headquarters several weeks prior to the primary election. "I am a big believer in reason and facts and evidence and science and feedback—everything that allows you to do what you do. That's what we should be doing in our government," Obama told the packed auditorium. "I think that many of you can help me, so I want you to be involved." He probably meant that he wanted donations, or maybe votes, but I took him literally. I took a leave of absence from Google initially and eventually quit my job to move from California to Chicago to join the campaign.

I joined what was being called the "new media" team. They used the phrase "new media" because it encompassed everything that didn't typically fit into traditional political campaigns: email, social media, blogging, SMS, and the web. The team had competent bloggers, designers, and email copywriters; I wondered where I might be able to make an impact.

One thing stood out to me: a red button.

Online donations to the campaign came from subscribers to the email newsletter; subscriptions for this came from the campaign website's signup form; and the signup form came as a result of clicking a red button that said "Sign Up." This was the gateway through which all of Obama's email supporters had to pass; it all came down to one button. So, one simple, humble question immediately became pivotal.

Is This the Right Button?

Is this our *best* chance to get every single supporter, and every single dollar, that we possibly can?

I had zero political experience at the time, and little clout within the organization. I didn't have a politico's intuition about what the button or the image above it should look like—nor the persuasive rhetoric required to run any proposed improvements up the chain of command. All I had was one insistent question: *Is this button the absolute best?*—and the desire to find the answer. There was only one way to know for certain.

Knowing little about politics or why certain words and images might be more moving or more effective than others, I suggested experimenting to figure out what worked to drive the most signups. Our team tested four different labels for the button ("Sign Up," "Sign Up Now," "Join Us Now," and "Learn More") and six different media (images and videos) above it to see which combination induced the most visitors to engage and sign up.

Our team took bets on which variation (Figures 1.1 through 1.3) would perform best at garnering email signups. Most folks put their money on "Sam's Video," a compilation of some of the most powerful moments in Obama's speeches. We assumed *any* video—with not just Obama's image, but his voice and message—would lead more people to enter their email addresses than a simple static image would.

Boy, were we wrong.

FIGURE 1.1 The original splash page we set out to optimize at the Obama campaign in 2008.

Source: Optimizely.

FIGURE 1.2 The button variations we tested.

Source: Optimizely.

IMAGES   VIDEOS

FIGURE 1.3   The media variations we tested.

Source: Optimizely.

ORIGINAL   VARIATION

FIGURE 1.4 A side-by-side comparison of the original and winning variation of the splash page at the 2008 Obama campaign.

Source: Optimizely.,

In fact, not only "Sam's Video" but *every* video dramatically underperformed *every* image. Even more dramatically, one image-and-button combination in particular stood head and shoulders above the original (Figure 1.4).

A combination of the "Family Image" and the "Learn More" button improved the signup rate by a staggering 40.6 percent. Over the course of the campaign, that 40.6 percent lift in signups translated to 2.8 million more email subscribers, 288,000 more volunteers, and—perhaps most important of all—an additional $57 *million* in donations.

Obama went on, with an enormous lead in dollars and supporters raised online, to win the election. He was buoyed by a team willing to *test everything* and to *listen to the data* even when it surprised them the most.

A small, simple question about a small red button had been answered conclusively with a straightforward experiment. But in its place loomed another question, just as simple and just as insistent:

"Why aren't more people doing this?"

The Age of Testing

The answer, in short, was that the commercially available tools at the time required heavy involvement from software engineers to run experiments. For all of the spectacular gains that website testing enabled at the Obama campaign— as well as at big-tech players like Google and Amazon—it was still a highly technical practice. It was simply out of reach for most businesses that didn't have the know-how and a dedicated in-house team, and prohibitively difficult even for many that did. But why did this have to remain the case? Why couldn't *every* organization have access to these tools?

I joined up with my fellow Google product manager, Pete Koomen, and in 2010 the two of us struck off on our own to help do just that. What we built as a result is Optimizely, a website optimization platform that makes it easy for *any* organization, from a one-person startup to a Fortune 100 firm, to do what the Obama team did on the road to the White House—with no degrees in statistics or dedicated engineering team required.

Over the past several years, a range of new tools has emerged to make this online testing and optimization practice—**A/B testing**, as it is known—easier and faster. The concept of A/B testing is simple: show different variations of your website to different people and measure which variation is the most effective at turning them into customers. If each visitor to your website is randomly shown one of these variations and you do this over the same period of time, then you've created a controlled experiment known as an *A/B test*. A/B testing has gone from a secret weapon within the purview of only a handful of tech companies to an increasingly ubiquitous and critical part of doing business online.

This sea change in the way companies are conducting online business and marketing is perhaps best illustrated by taking a glance at the election cycle that came next: the 2012 presidential race. There were some key differences between 2012 and 2008: the Obama campaign team had an intense testing program in place from day one and didn't need to be persuaded as to the mission-critical value of A/B testing. The other key difference: so did the opponent, Mitt Romney.

Leading publications from *TIME* to *The Atlantic* to *Businessweek* to *Forbes* wrote about the 2012 presidential campaign fundraising machines as being the most sophisticated, data-driven, and efficient organizations that politics had ever seen. And at the heart of this new reality was A/B testing.

Optimization for Everyone

Whether or not you have plans to run for office in the near future, whether you come from a huge organization or a team of one, and whether your background is in computer science or marketing, *you can make these same changes happen* in your own workplace.

In this book we'll tell the story of a number of different companies—what they tested, what they learned, and how testing has grown to become part of their mindset, values, and culture. We at Optimizely have been fortunate to witness this transformation take place time and again. Part of what we want to change is the notion that testing is something that only IT staff or developers can do, because nothing could be further from the truth. Anyone can conduct A/B testing, and it can affect—and infect—an entire organization.

This book is for anyone interested in building a culture of testing within his or her organization by being curious enough, brave enough, and humble enough to ask simple questions like "Is this red button the best?" and to experiment to find the answer. Through our experiences building Optimizely and through extensive contact with our own customers, we've come to understand very well the challenges that this group faces—a group that includes the following members at its core:

- Digital marketers and marketing managers
- Designers
- Product managers
- Software engineers
- Entrepreneurs
- Copywriters
- Growth hackers
- Data scientists

No matter your role or experience level, your seniority or budget, you'll come away from this book with a host of new ideas, as well as a seasoned understanding of the challenges—and advantages—involved in using data to drive your organization's growth and revenue. To help you get going, we'll start with some of the most common questions:

"How should we choose what to test?"

"How can my team and I adopt a sustainable testing process?"

"Where do we begin?"

This book takes you through dozens of real-world examples that show specifically how teams like yours have embraced A/B testing as a fundamental part of not only their day-to-day workflow, but their *creative* process as well. We examine dramatic successes, subtle differences, and surprising failures, and we reveal a wealth of ideas and actionable insights by looking through the eyes of the people and teams who discovered them.

Each case study serves to highlight different best (and worst) practices, and we've grouped our studies broadly based on common underlying themes. You can read them one after the other, or pick and choose targeted examples based on what you're looking for. At the end of each chapter, we've included a brisk "TL;DR" (too long; didn't read) condensation of the chapter's main points and key takeaways.

The tools are out there, and they're not hard to get or hard to use. All you need to do is start asking questions. Who knows where they might lead you?

Lessons Learned from 200,000 A/B Tests (and Counting)

Having worked with thousands of different organizations on hundreds of thousands of different A/B tests, we've been able to distill some of the key principles and insights that any tester or testing team should have in mind as they make their first forays into testing. Part I addresses some of the typical questions that you might have about jumping in, starting with perhaps the biggest: "Where do I begin?"

And that's exactly where we pick up next.

What to Test

Optimization in Five Steps

The hardest part of A/B testing is determining what to test in the first place. Having worked with thousands of customers who do A/B testing every day, one of the most common questions we hear is, "Where do I begin?"

A mistake that some companies make is to start moving a bunch of levers around without clear planning upfront for what they're trying to optimize—and what will be impacted by those changes. It's tempting to just dive in and start changing parts of your homepage, or your product page, or your checkout page, without truly understanding the value that it's generating (or not generating) for your business.

Instead, we advise a purposeful and deliberate five-step process:

Step One: Define success
Step Two: Identify bottlenecks
Step Three: Construct a hypothesis
Step Four: Prioritize
Step Five: Test

This process begins with the most important question of all: *What is the purpose of your site?*

Step One: Define Success

Before you can determine which of your test's variations is the winner, you have to first decide how you're keeping score. To start A/B testing successfully, you need to answer a specific question: What is your website for? If you could make your website do *one* thing better, what would it do?

If the answer to that question isn't completely clear to you, there's a trick that might help. Imagine the following dialogue:

ALICE: "What do you want to achieve with A/B testing?"

BOB: "We don't know. We don't know what we want our website to do."

ALICE: "Why don't you take it down?"

BOB: "Of course not! We need our website because it—"

And then Bob has the *aha!* moment that crystallizes his website's *raison d'être*: He can see reasons for the website deeper than "Everyone else has one, so we need one, too."

Defining success in the context of A/B testing involves taking the answer to the question of your site's ultimate purpose and turning it into something more precise: *quantifiable success metrics*. Your success metrics are the specific numbers you hope will be improved by your tests.

It's fairly easy for an e-commerce business to define its success metrics in terms of revenue per visitor (though there are complexities and "gotchas" we'll discuss later), and for a fundraising website to define its success metrics in terms of average donation per visitor. Depending on your business model, defining your success metrics may be trickier.

For instance, Google's search engineers measure what they call *abandonment*, which is when a user leaves a search results page without clicking anything. Abandonment can be bad—perhaps none of the results looked helpful—but it can also be good—perhaps the results page itself was so informative that there was no need to click through to any of the pages.

SITE TYPE	COMMON CONVERSION & AGGREGATE GOALS
E-Commerce A site that sells things for users to purchase online.	• Completed purchase • Each step within the checkout funnel • Products added to cart • Product page views
Media/Content A site focused on article or other content consumption.	• Page views • Articles read • Bounce rate (when measuring within an A/B testing tool, this is often measured by seeing if the user clicked anywhere on the page)
Lead Generation A site that acquires business through name capture.	• Form completion • Clicks to a form page (links may read "Contact Us" for example)
Donation A site aiming to collect donations.	• Form completion • Clicks to a form page (links may read "Send a donation" for example)

FIGURE 2.1   Table of conversion goals by site type.

Figure 2.1 lists some of the most common success metrics for particular site types. Here we've broken websites down into four broad categories.

Part of building out your testing strategy is identifying what constitutes—and does not constitute—a "conversion" for your particular site. In online terms, a conversion is the point at which a visitor takes the desired action on your website. Pinpointing the specific actions you want people to take most on your site and that are most critical to your business will lead you to the tests that have an impact.

Macroconversions, Microconversions, and Vanity Metrics

Author and digital marketing evangelist Avinash Kaushik makes the distinction between what he calls *macroconversions*—the metric most closely aligned with your site's primary raison d'être, as we discussed earlier—and *microconversions*—the other actions that users take on your site. While microconversions (things like clicking one button in a signup funnel, watching a video, or commenting on a blog post) may not be as immediately valuable or monetizeable as macroconversions, they can provide a tremendous amount of *indirect* value (provided they're not optimized at the expense of macroconversions).

A quick word of caution: sometimes a business can be lured into chasing "vanity metrics" that end up being distractions from the actual goal.

Consider a hypothetical business-to-business (B2B) software company's blog. The marketing team wants the blog to be a hub of thought leadership in their industry. Since they're A/B testing the main site, they decide to start optimizing the blog, too. On the main site, their aim is clear: to use A/B testing to help drive more free trial signups. Defining quantifiable goals for the blog is harder for the team, so they have been unable to define what makes an A/B test *successful*.

For the B2B blog, a vanity metric could be headline clicks. If this is the only piece of data you're using to determine whether the blog is successful, you could be optimizing the wrong thing. Maybe people click headlines because they are shocking, but don't read past them. If all you measure is clicks, you'll never know whether the content of the actual post is good. More telling metrics might be call-to-action clicks, comments, shares, and repeat visits.

Of course, at the end of the day, "thought leadership" is successful only when it results in incremental revenue for the business, but this is very difficult to measure directly. Without clearly defined goals for your site, it's tempting to focus on and optimize for vanity metrics: data that can seem impressive, but doesn't really matter to what you are trying to achieve.

Step Two: Identify Bottlenecks

Once you've determined what your site's quantifiable success metrics are, you can turn your attention to your site analytics and discover where your biggest *bottlenecks* are: the places where your users are dropping off, or the places where you're losing the most momentum in moving users through your desired series of actions.

> DAN: At the Obama campaign in November 2007, before the Iowa caucuses took place, and before our website had much traffic or traction, we did notice one thing by looking at Google Analytics for our user funnel (Figure 2.2).

We had a bunch of people visiting the site—mostly organically—but we also had a very efficient paid marketing campaign. And we were also doing really well getting people to donate once we had their email addresses. The bottleneck was in convincing our site visitors to sign up for our email list (Figure 2.3).

This in turn helped us understand that we had a big opportunity to optimize the email signup step.

The 2008 Obama campaign page generated roughly 10 million email subscriptions, and the lift from the landing page experiment brought in an additional 2.8 million email addresses. Ten percent of the people on our email list volunteered, which meant another 280,000 volunteers. What is perhaps most impressive, and

FIGURE 2.2 Path of the assumed fundraising funnel for the Obama 2008 campaign.

FIGURE 2.3 Path of the actual fundraising funnel at the campaign. High volume of visitors to the site but there's significant dropoff in the email signup step.

most relevant to web businesses, is the lift in terms of the *amount raised*. Because we defined quantifiable success metrics—and knew that we did a great job of raising money from people once we had their email addresses—we had a hunch that if we just got a bunch more email addresses, we'd raise much more money. And sure enough, we raised an additional $57 million.

The Obama example also highlights another equally important part of identifying quantifiable success metrics: agreeing on them. There was a widely held belief inside the campaign at the time that a video would be the most effective media choice for the barackobama.com landing page, and it was only after the team agreed on the definition of *effective* that an objective decision could be made. (We'll explore A/B testing and office decision-making culture further in Chapter 8.)

Step Three: Construct a Hypothesis

Once you've identified what the bottlenecks are in your process, use your understanding of visitor intent to come up with test hypotheses. Consider different forms of qualitative research such as user interviews, feedback forms, or focus groups to gain an understanding of what's going on in users' heads as they interact with your site.

In January 2010, the second-deadliest earthquake ever recorded struck near Léogâne, Haiti. A massive global aid effort began almost instantly, and within days, former presidents Bill Clinton and George W. Bush had established the Clinton Bush Haiti Fund to raise money and support for the relief effort. Time was of the essence and the organization quickly created a simple donation page to collect donations from the millions of visitors the site was seeing every day, thanks to a massive media and press campaign.

The organization was vastly under-resourced at the beginning; they had one extremely overworked IT person who was in charge of the whole operation, and he had barely enough time to make sure the servers were running. (Building a site capable of handling millions of visitors in just a few days is no small feat.) The team at the Clinton Foundation responsible for the website called and said, "Can you help us?"

The donation page was a fertile place for A/B testing to make a big difference: a hastily designed, high-traffic page with a clear conversion goal (Figure 2.4). However, we knew the situation wouldn't last forever, so we really had to hustle in order to make a difference.

We spent three days and nights not only building a series of tests but actually building the scaffolding that would enable us to *run* the tests, effectively constructing the airplane in midflight.

We chose our success metric carefully. We didn't want to optimize for percentage of users making donations, nor for average donation amount, since an increase in one metric might easily be achieved at the expense of the other. The success metric we decided on was dollars per pageview, which was the average amount of money the organization was making per pair of eyeballs seeing this page. We settled on this metric as the best choice to optimize for value to the organization.

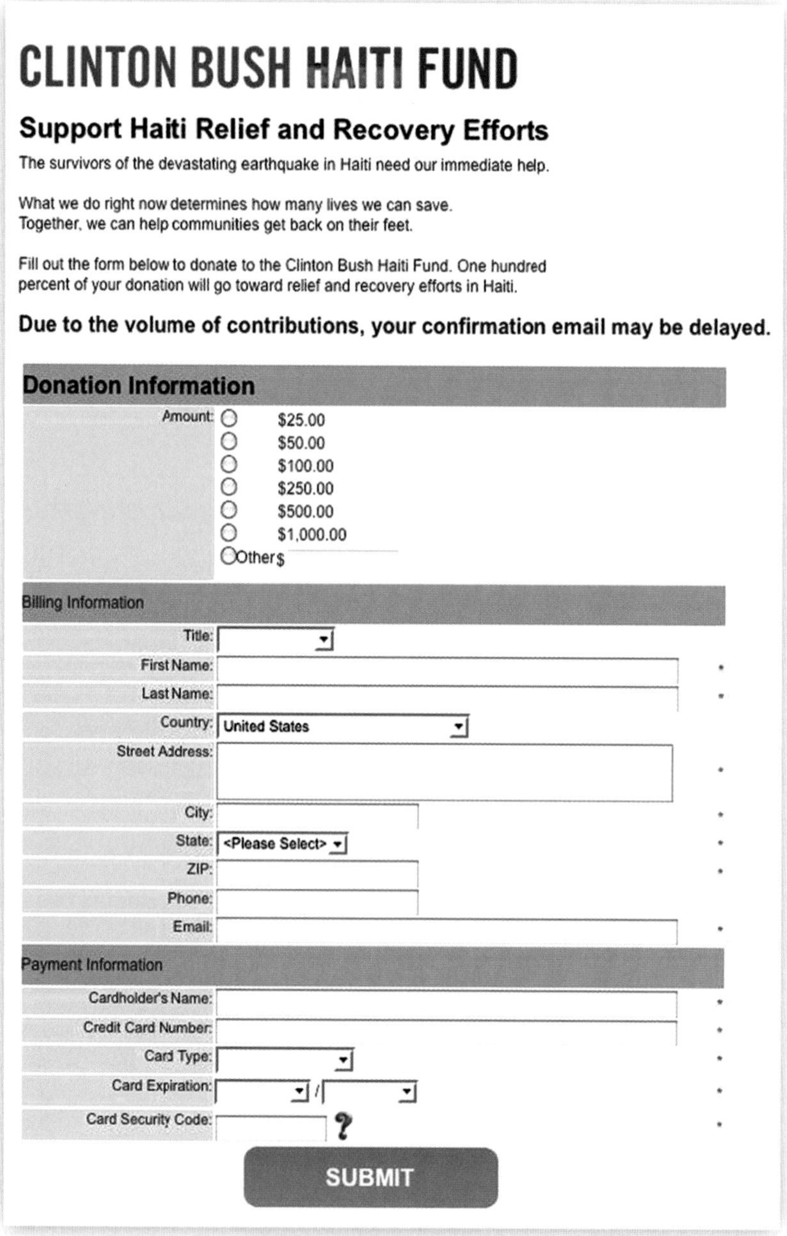

CLINTON BUSH HAITI FUND

Support Haiti Relief and Recovery Efforts

The survivors of the devastating earthquake in Haiti need our immediate help.

What we do right now determines how many lives we can save.
Together, we can help communities get back on their feet.

Fill out the form below to donate to the Clinton Bush Haiti Fund. One hundred percent of your donation will go toward relief and recovery efforts in Haiti.

Due to the volume of contributions, your confirmation email may be delayed.

Donation Information

Amount: ○ $25.00
○ $50.00
○ $100.00
○ $250.00
○ $500.00
○ $1,000.00
○ Other $ _____

Billing Information

Title: [▾]
First Name: [ ] *
Last Name: [ ] *
Country: [United States ▾]
Street Address: [ ] *
City: [ ] *
State: [<Please Select> ▾] *
ZIP: [ ] *
Phone: [ ]
Email: [ ] *

Payment Information

Cardholder's Name: [ ] *
Credit Card Number: [ ] *
Card Type: [▾] *
Card Expiration: [▾] / [▾] *
Card Security Code: [ ] ? *

SUBMIT

FIGURE 2.4   The initial Clinton Bush Haiti Fund page.

Armed with our metric, we next had to identify where the optimizable areas of the site were. What was the major bottleneck holding back donations? Traffic *to* the site wasn't the problem; we could hardly handle the load. And the site itself was little more than a single page with a donation form, so the bottleneck must be part of the donation page itself.

The initial donation page was essentially a long form, consisting of lots of blank spaces on a white background. We tried to put ourselves inside the visitors' heads, and from their perspective we hypothesized that the form-only page might seem overly abstract. We hypothesized that adding an image of earthquake victims would make the form more concrete and emotive, spurring more visitors to make donations and to make larger donations (Figure 2.5).

Surprisingly, when we tested a variation page with an image against the original, we saw our average donation per pageview go *down*. Here's the point in a testing process where having a hypothesis is critical. Had we simply been trying things at random, we could have easily stopped sending traffic to that variation and never investigated any further. But looking more closely at the page with the image on it led us to a *second* hypothesis: maybe the loss in donations wasn't due to the image itself, but due to the fact that the image was pushing the form down the page ("below the fold"), requiring users to scroll.

What would happen, we hypothesized, if we adopted a two-column layout and put the image *beside* the form? This test would help us make sense of our previous result: whether it was the image itself lowering our metrics, or the layout (Figure 2.6).

It turned out that this layout brought in significantly more donations than not only the failing one-column-with-image layout, but, more importantly and more rewardingly, the original form as well. This new layout (along with several other

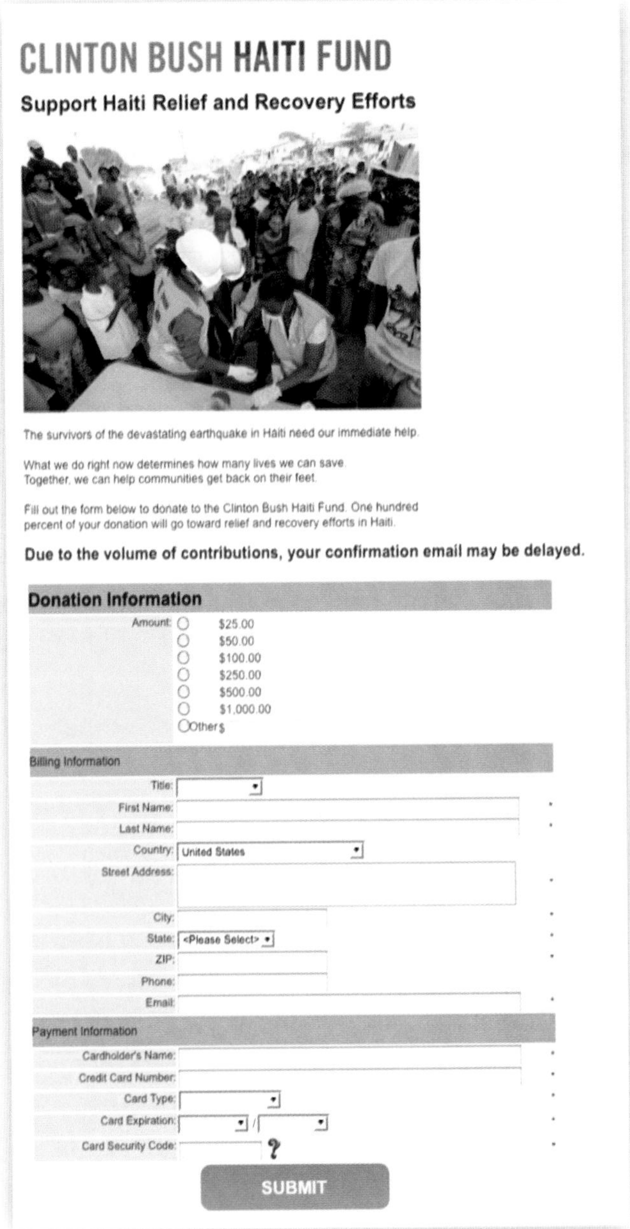

FIGURE 2.5   The Clinton Bush Haiti Fund page with image added.

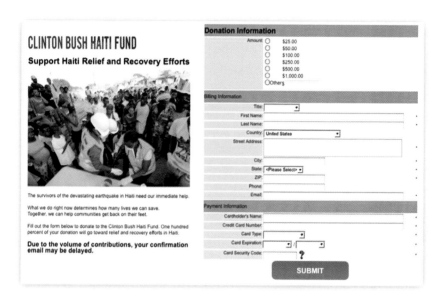

FIGURE 2.6   The Clinton Bush Haiti Fund page with two-column layout.

optimizations that we'll discuss in the chapters to come) led to over a million dollars of additional relief aid for Haiti.

Hypotheses make tests more informative because they provide a specific purpose by helping you hone in on what you are actually trying to determine. If you run an experiment without forming a hypothesis beforehand, you might gather information that's helpful anecdotally while missing the deeper lesson. Experimentation inherently generates more questions than it answers, and when used effectively will always validate or invalidate some hypothesis, thus lending focus to the next round of questions.

"Failed" tests are valuable because they often lead to new hypotheses for why they didn't turn out the way you expected. Generating these hypotheses is sometimes tricky, because visitors behave in complex ways. Regardless of the complexity, however, employing the scientific method in testing will bring you closer to a meaningful understanding of your website's audience.

"With a disaster like the Haiti earthquake, every second counts when it comes to attracting donations, and it goes without saying that every dollar counts," said Marie Ewald, Director of Online Fundraising for the Clinton Foundation. "In less than 48 hours we tested eight versions of the donation page, and through this experiment we were able to generate an additional $1,022,571 in online revenue."

Step Four: Prioritize

Once you've generated hypotheses about user behavior that lead to candidate page variations for testing, you'll need to use your intuition about what's going to have the biggest impact to rank-order your experiments.

"Use ROI [return on investment] to prioritize your tests," says Kyle Rush, who was the Deputy Director of Frontend Web Development at Obama for America. "That's one of the biggest things I've learned in my career."

In a perfect world, you might test absolutely everything, but no team in the real world operates without constraints; your team's attention, budget, time, and also your site's traffic are all finite. These realities make prioritization of testing hypotheses a necessity.

For your very first test, there may be extra considerations, such as wanting to secure the buy-in of others within your organization, or not wanting to try overly elaborate test integrations on a new platform. We'll explore these pragmatic concerns more deeply in Chapter 8. The important thing to bear in mind overall, however, is keeping a sense of your testing priorities. Your projected ROI from each test will itself be derived from a combination of your core success metrics (Step One), the bottlenecks in your conversion funnel (Step Two), and your hypotheses about your users' behavior (Step Three).

Step Five: Test

All that's left is to run the test. You'll show randomly selected visitors the variation(s) and track how they behave relative to users seeing the current site with respect to the quantifiable success metrics you've determined. (We'll discuss the decision process for choosing the right testing platform in Chapter 7.)

Once the test reaches statistical significance, you'll have your answer. (See Appendix 2 for more information on the mathematics of statistical significance, and the best practices for how long to let a test run.)

Often a completed test yields not only answers, but—as in any other science—more questions. And this cycle of iteration, of exploration and refinement, is exactly where we pick up in Chapter 3.

TL;DR

- You can't pick a winner until you decide how you're keeping score. A/B testing starts with determining **quantifiable success metrics**.

- There are a number of possible **conversion goals**: time on site, pageviews, average order value, revenue per visitor, and so on. Take the time to pick the one that's right for you.

- Site analytics along with your own instincts will suggest **bottlenecks** where you can focus your attention.

- Understanding visitor intent with the help of interviews and usability tests will suggest **hypotheses** about what to change and how.

- **Prioritize** your experiments based on your prediction of their impact.

- **Start testing**, and continue until you begin to see diminishing returns.

Seek the Global Maximum

Refinement and Exploration

Premature optimization is the root of all evil.

Donald Knuth

Imagine you're climbing a mountain: if your goal is to get to the top of the *tallest* mountain, and you don't have a map of the range, it's probably not a good idea just to start walking up the nearest slope. You'll climb, and climb, and then ultimately reach some peak—and then what? Where do you move next if this peak doesn't turn out to be the highest one?

In optimization, the term for the nearby, uphill peak is the *local maximum*, whereas the distant, largest peak is the *global maximum*.

One of the things that we like to tell companies that we work with is to be willing to *think big*. Being too complacent about the status quo can lead to focusing too much on fine-tuning. As Figure 3.1 highlights, the "Refinement" path might lead you to miss out on the best solution that could have been discovered with the "Exploration" approach. While refinement can lead to a solution better than what you have today, we recommend exploring multiple alternatives that might not resemble the current site first. We encourage the kind of humility and bravery required to say, "You know, the website we have today is far from perfect. Let's try some *dramatically* new layouts, new designs, and redesigns, figure out which of those work well, and *then* refine from there."

However, it's not as simple as saying that one should always explore first and always refine second. The truth is that exploration and refinement are complementary techniques, and most effective when used in tandem. Often the process of using

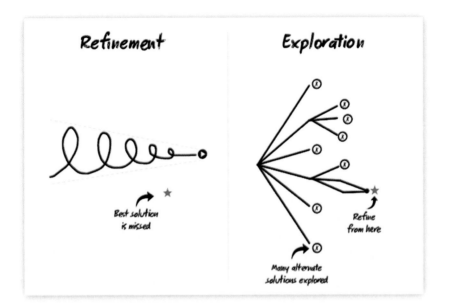

FIGURE 3.1   Refinement and exploration.
Source: Intercom.

hypothesis testing for refinement produces key insights that can deeply inform the redesign. In other words, sometimes you need to get above the tree line to see where the bigger peak lies.

As the following case studies reveal, there are huge wins to be had from thinking big and being open to questioning the status quo. There are also important revelations lurking in smaller tests that can point the way to a major redesign. And sometimes testing is the only way to find true north amidst the chaos and confusion of major changes.

Break from the Status Quo: ABC Family

Disney ran an experiment using Optimizely on the ABC Family homepage.

FIGURE 3.2 ABC Family A/B test: original.

The page (shown in Figure 3.2) displayed a large promotion for a television show you might be interested in. After looking through their search logs, however, the Disney digital team discovered that a lot of people were searching for the exact titles of shows and specific episodes. Instead of taking the incremental approach (e.g., by tweaking the promo image, or rotating the featured show), the team decided to reevaluate their entire approach. They created an alternative view, one that was less visual and more hierarchical, in which users can drill down through menus to specific shows (Figure 3.3).

FIGURE 3.3 ABC Family A/B test: variation.

Disney had defined as their quantifiable success metric the percentage of visitors who clicked on any part of the experiment page. Their goal was to lift this engagement by 10 to 20 percent. In fact, by being open to this big, fundamental change, they were able to effect an engagement increase of more than *600 percent.*

Learn Your Way to the New Site: Chrome Industries

Kyle Duford at cycling bag and apparel manufacturer Chrome Industries explains that the Chrome team is presently discussing a major site redesign. "We're purposely using all of these tests to formulate how we approach the new website."

The Chrome team discovered something surprising when they were A/B testing the order of the three promotional content blocks on their homepage: the content they put in the center block seemed *always* to outperform the content they put in the left block (Figure 3.4).

The team's assumption was that because people read from left to right, they would explore in this manner. "This is gold," says Duford. Now they know to put their most important promo block in the center, but the bigger lesson is that users seem to go straight for the central imagery, rather than scanning left to right. This is a valuable insight that may end up altering the entire new layout for the site redesign. "The look and feel will be completely different, but the ideas of the blocks of content that go into it are all being discovered through this process," Duford says. "So while it's important right now to understand how people shop, it's more important because it's going to inform our decisions going forward."

ORIGINAL

VARIATION

FIGURE 3.4   Chrome Industries promo block test—middle block most clicked, regardless of content.

Rethink the Business Model: Lumosity

Lumosity is a company that offers web-based games designed to improve users' minds. Their business model is simple: users pay a monthly subscription fee to access games designed by neuroscientists to promote cognitive function. Users derive the most benefit from training regularly, and boosting user engagement was an important goal. What wasn't intuitive, however, was what the Lumosity development team did to increase this metric.

Lumosity's scientists recommended that users train for 15 to 20 minutes a day, 4 to 5 times per week—not unlike physical exercise—although the site didn't actually constrain users to a specific time limit. The data showed that people would stay logged in for many hours, but that over time, the frequency of logins declined, suggesting users were burning out.

The team hypothesized that limiting the amount of training a user could do in one day would improve engagement over time.

Giving users one training session a day and congratulating them on being done for the day might achieve their goal. Such a radical change initially made many people at the company nervous, including Product Manager Eric Dorf, who feared that restricting the amount of a time a user could use the service they were paying for would frustrate the user base. "I felt like, if I'm paying for this as a subscription and I'm not allowed to train as much as I want, why would I pay for it?" he says. "I remember thinking, 'Gosh, I hope we don't piss everybody off.'"

Trying out the new model as part of an A/B test mitigated that risk. The team ran an A/B test that set the original, unlimited training against the limited-training variation (Figures 3.5 and 3.6). The results shocked Eric and his team. Users actually trained more over time in the new model. "The graph was so clear," Eric says. "People were training more as a result of being limited."

After making this discovery, the Lumosity team changed the way they position, build, and sell their program. The message of daily training is the cornerstone of their communications to users. After this initial exploration, the team then subsequently used A/B testing to refine the approach, finding the messages and marketing that best support and reinforce the idea of daily training.

Today, when a user completes a session, the message is, "You're done. You can leave the site now," Dorf explains. "It's not like a lot of other gaming products that want you to spend all your time playing. The scientists are happy because more users are more engaged with training than before."

Test *Through* the Redesign, Not After: Digg and Netflix

When it comes to making better data-driven decisions, the sooner the better. Often the temptation is (and we've heard this before)

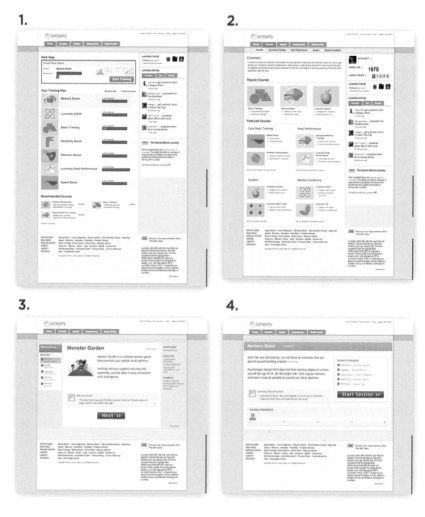

FIGURE 3.5 Original Lumosity user experience—unlimited daily training.

"Oh, we're doing a redesign; we'll do the A/B testing afterwards." The fact is you actually want to *A/B test the redesign*.

Around 2010, we were introduced to the folks at Digg by their new VP of Product Keval Desai to talk about using Optimizely. Their response was, "We are busy working on a complete overhaul of our site. After we do that, then we'll do A/B testing."

FIGURE 3.6   New Lumosity user experience—limited daily training.

As Desai explains, the "Digg v4" redesign was a perfect storm of problems. The company rolled out a new backend and a new frontend at the same time, conflating two different sets of challenges. "It was a big bang launch," he says. The backend couldn't initially handle the site traffic and buckled on launch day. What's more, despite faring well in usability tests, focus groups, surveys, and a private beta, the new frontend met with vociferous criticism when it was released to the public, and became a magnet for negative media attention. "When you change something, people are going to have a reaction," Desai says. "Most of the changes, I would say, were done for the right reasons, and I think that eventually the community settled down despite the initial uproar." But, he says, "a big-bang launch in today's era of continuous development is just a bad idea." "To me, that's the power of A/B testing: that you can make this big bet but reduce the risk out of it as much as possible by incrementally testing each new feature," Desai explains. People are naturally resistant to change, so almost any major site redesign is guaranteed to get user pushback. The difference is that A/B testing the new design should reveal whether it's *actually* hurting or helping the core success metrics of the site. "You can't [always] prevent the user backlash. But you can know you did the right thing."

Netflix offers a similar story of a rocky redesign, but with a crucial difference: they were A/B testing the new layout, and had the numbers to stand tall against user flak. In June 2011, Netflix announced a new "look and feel" to the Watch Instantly web interface. "Starting today," wrote Director of Product Management Michael Spiegelman on the company's blog, "most members who watch instantly will see a new interface that provides more focus on the TV shows and movies streaming from Netflix." At the time of writing, the most liked comment under the short post reads, "New Netflix interface is complete crap," followed by a litany of similarly critical comments. The interface Netflix released to its 24 million members on that day is the same design you see today on netflix.com: personalized scrollable rows of titles that Netflix has calculated you will like best. So, in the face of some bad press on the blogosphere, why did Netflix decide to keep the new design? The answer is clear to Netflix Manager of Experimentation Bryan Gumm, who worked on that redesign: the data simply said so.

The team began working on the interface redesign in January 2011. They called the project "Density," because the new design's goal was literally a denser user experience (Figure 3.7).

The original experience had given the user four titles in a row from which to choose, with a "play" button and star rating under each title's thumbnail. Each title also had ample whitespace surrounding it—a waste of screen real estate, in the team's opinion.

The variation presented scrollable rows with title thumbnails. The designers removed the star rating and play button from the default view, and made it a hover experience instead.

They then A/B tested both variations on a small subset of new and existing members while measuring retention and engagement in both variations. The result: retention in the

ORIGINAL  VARIATION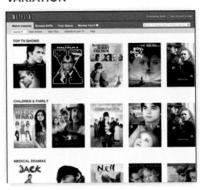

FIGURE 3.7 Netflix original site versus "Density" redesign.

variation increased by 20 to 55 basis points, and engagement grew by 30 to 140 basis points.

The data clearly told the designers that new and existing members preferred the variation to the original. Netflix counted it as a success and rolled the new "density" interface out to 100 percent of its users in June 2011. As Gumm asserts, "If [the results hadn't been] positive, we wouldn't have rolled it out." The company measured engagement and retention again in the rollout as a gut-check. Sure enough, the results of the second test concurred with the first that users watched more movies and TV shows with the new interface.

Then the comment backlash started.

However, as far as Netflix is concerned, the metrics reflecting data from existing and new members tell the absolute truth. As Gumm explains, the vocal minority made up a small fraction of the user base and they voiced an opinion that went against all the data Netflix had about the experience. Gumm points out, "We were looking at the metrics and people were watching more, they liked it better, and they were more engaged in the service. . . . [Both the tests] proved it."

Gumm also makes the following very important point: "What people say and what they do are rarely the same. We're not going to tailor the product experience, just like we're not going to have 80 million different engineering paths, just to please half a percent of the people. It's just not worth the support required."

Gumm then reminds us that despite the few loud, unhappy customers that may emerge, the most critical thing to remember is the data: "I think it's really important in an A/B testing organization, or any data-driven organization, to just hold true to the philosophy that the *data is what matters.*"

TL;DR

- Incrementalism can lead to local maxima. Be willing to **explore** to find the big wins before testing smaller changes and tweaks.

- Conversely, sometimes it's the incremental refinements that prove or disprove your hypotheses about what your users respond to. **Use the insights from small tests** to guide and inform your thinking about bigger changes.

- Consider entirely new **alternative approaches** to your principal business goals. Be willing to go beyond just testing "variations on a theme"—you might be surprised.

- If you're working on a major site redesign or overhaul, don't wait until the new design is live to A/B test it. **A/B test the redesign** itself.

Less Is More: Reduce Choices

When Subtraction Adds Value

Sometimes the winning variation of a page is one in which you haven't added anything at all but in fact *removed* elements from the page. We have seen many teams improve conversion metrics simply by adhering to the design mantra "Less is more." The products of this approach—simpler pages, shorter forms, and fewer choices—can make a very big difference.

Every Field Counts: The Clinton Bush Haiti Fund

In Chapter 2 we discussed one of the most significant tests we ran with the Clinton Bush Haiti Fund: adding an image and shifting to a two-column layout.

Another one of our hypotheses had to do with the actual donation form itself. When you're asking the user to take an action, every bit of effort counts, and so we wanted to look at the form to see if there was any way we could streamline the user's experience. We noticed that the Foundation had included fields for "phone number" and "title," hoping down the road to be able to use this information, possibly to make phone solicitations. The fact was, however, that the Foundation was stretched so thin that it wasn't actually calling anyone, so this additional information being requested of users wasn't being put to use. We hypothesized that getting rid of these two optional fields, even if it came at the cost of some potentially useful data, would be more than made up for by added donations in virtue of the simpler form (Figure 4.1).

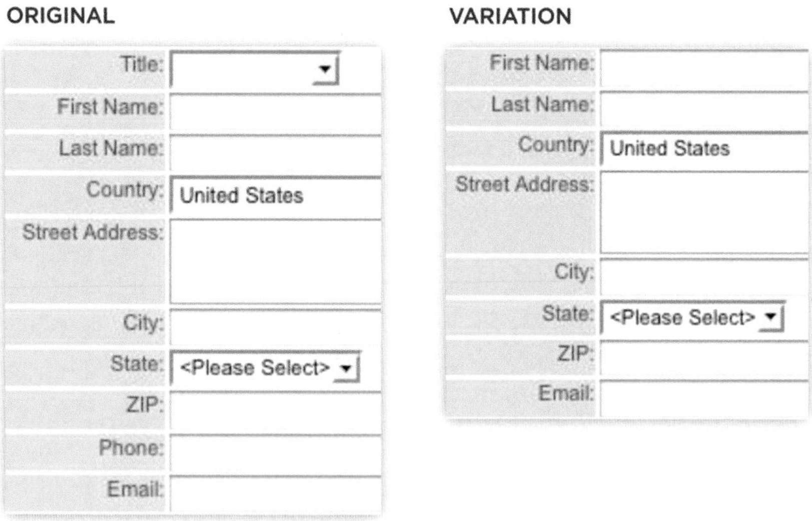

FIGURE 4.1   Original donation form versus form with optional fields removed.

The effect was instantly measurable and dramatic. Simply removing two optional fields resulted in an 11 percent improvement in dollars per pageview over the length of the test—a massive gain in donations from a small simplification.

Keep It Simple: SeeClickFix

SeeClickFix is a web tool that allows citizens to "report neighborhood issues, and see them get fixed." The tool centers on a web-based map that displays user activity. Users add comments, suggest resolutions, and add video and picture documentation. Anyone can elect to receive email alerts based on "Watch Areas" by geographical area and can filter reports by keyword.

The original SeeClickFix homepage contained a simple call to action with one form and a simple design.

After a great deal of work by the team's designers and engineers, SeeClickFix had a brand-new homepage ready to launch, complete with an interactive map (Figure 4.2). The

ORIGINAL

VARIATION

FIGURE 4.2 Original SeeClickFix homepage versus redesigned map homepage.

team was excited about it, and used an A/B test to find out just how brilliant their new design idea was.

They were in for a surprise. SeeClickFix actually drove *8 percent more* engagement on the simple gray box form that displayed a simple call to action and a description. The proposed new homepage may have been more technologically sophisticated and visually rich, but *simplicity mattered* where it counted most: getting visitors to engage with the site.

Hide Options: Cost Plus World Market

The checkout funnel is a prime place for optimization on a site, and a place where it's often true that less is more. This makes intuitive sense: nonessential steps included in the purchase process can be distracting, and it's no surprise that minimizing obstacles frequently boosts conversion. What's interesting is that removing unnecessary *options* can also reduce the overall friction of the process in a significant way.

Cost Plus World Market, a chain of specialty/import retail stores and a subsidiary of Bed Bath & Beyond, ran an experiment that tested hiding the promotion code and shipping options form fields from the last page in the checkout funnel (Figure 4.3).

By hiding these two optional fields and making them expandable links instead, Cost Plus saw a 15.6 percent increase in revenue per visitor. Conversions also went up by 5.2 percent in the variation with hidden fields.

Remove Distractions and "Outs": Avalanche Technology Group

It's important to remember that *any* clickable element on a page represents an option for your user, not just those explicitly

FIGURE 4.3   Cost Plus World Market original checkout page versus variation.

included in the checkout process. Our next example illustrates how valuable it can be to focus on those elements that aren't actually part of the checkout process.

Avalanche Technology Group is the Australian distributor for popular antivirus software AVG. When they examined their shopping cart conversion data they suspected there was room for improvement, and wanted to experiment with some "minor" (or so they thought) variations that would leave the actual steps of the checkout process untouched.

The team decided to run an experiment in which the site's header navigation links were removed from the checkout funnel, which they hypothesized would reduce visual noise and keep traffic more focused on actually checking out (Figure 4.4).

FIGURE 4.4   Original AVG checkout page versus variation.

This change alone improved conversion rates by 10 percent and led to a 16 percent increase in revenue per visitor, showing that even visually minor changes to the "auxiliary" parts of a page can have a big impact on visitor behavior.

Lower the Slope: Obama 2012

The previous examples show the potential benefits of keeping things simple by removing distractions and minimizing options. But how do you optimize when things are already as simple as they can possibly be? Or *are* they?

Every one of the 165 people on Obama's 2012 digital team understood how mission-critical A/B testing was to running the digital campaign. "We didn't have to convince anybody that A/B testing was important; it was just a no-brainer," recalls Kyle Rush, one of the lead developers on the campaign, who was responsible for much of the testing program.

The Obama 2012 team executed nearly 500 A/B tests over a 20-month period. The team experimented with everything from imagery and design to copy and usability. As a result, the optimization program collectively brought in an extra $190 million in campaign donations. One of the key tests that contributed to the $190 million pot was what came to be known as "Sequential."

The original donation process was a single page with a form and a picture of the president playing basketball. This page was already highly optimized: the image had been tested and not one superfluous form field existed—only the legally required ones remained. It looked pretty, and it was converting, but the campaign team wanted to see if they could go further. Since federal law requires specific information from campaign donors, the team couldn't just eliminate form fields at will. On the other hand, they

ORIGINAL

VARIATION

FIGURE 4.5   Original Obama 2012 campaign donation form versus variation with "Sequential" design.

Source: Kyle Rush.

knew from usability tests that the form was too long and losing potential donations. What to do? The team had an idea: make the form *appear* shorter by breaking it into pieces (Figure 4.5).

Once the form was divided into a sequence, the next logical thing to test was the *order* of the sequence. "Asking for the donation amount first more closely matches the users' state of mind," Rush explains. "Once they've made the decision to donate they're ready to enter an amount, not their personal information." Optimizations to the sequencing confirmed that donation amount should come first, then personal information, then billing, and occupation/employer last.

The optimized form yielded a 5 percent conversion increase over what had initially seemed to be the maximally optimized page. As Rush puts it: "You can get more users to the top of the mountain if you show them a gradual incline instead of a steep slope."

TL;DR

- More technologically or visually impressive pages don't necessarily lead to the user behavior you want. Experiment with **keeping it simple** and make any additional complexity earn its keep in your key success metrics.

- Every form field that users have to fill out is one more point of resistance between them and their conversion. Consider **deleting optional fields** and seeing if that lifts conversion.

- Giving visitors fewer distractions and fewer chances to leave the checkout funnel by **removing choices** can help boost conversion rates.

- Long forms have high risk for conversion failure. **Breaking up a long form** with required fields into multiple pages can increase chances for conversion.

5

Words Matter: Focus on Your Call to Action

How a Few Words Can Make a Huge Difference

The wording on your site represents an area where there are virtually inexhaustible opportunities for experimenting with variations. The variations can be crafted with just a few keystrokes, and often the slightest change can have a major effect. Because language is so easily tweaked (compared to art or images, which require careful design work) and its possibilities are so vast, it represents a major opportunity to test variations at the speed of brainstorming itself. The words on a site are some of the most powerful and potent elements a user sees. The right combination can be leaps-and-bounds more effective than the rest.

Reconsider "Submit": The Clinton Bush Haiti Fund

After we had been able to dramatically increase the donations per pageview at the Clinton Bush Haiti Fund by removing two of the form fields, we next considered the call-to-action button itself, and asked ourselves if the word "Submit" was really putting our best foot forward.

Instead we tried the label "Support Haiti," hypothesizing that making the button reflect the purpose of their action would make the *meaning* of their clicks more immediately clear to users (Figure 5.1).

The difference was enormous. The effect of the change from "Submit" to "Support Haiti" was on the order of several dollars per pageview, and this small change, together with our optimizations to

ORIGINAL VARIATION

FIGURE 5.1 Original donation form call-to-action copy versus variation.

the form and several other quick, simple tests, managed to bring in an additional million dollars of relief aid to Haiti. It's a testament to the power just one or two words can have.

Find the Perfect Appeal: Wikipedia

While the content on Wikipedia is the result of a vast collective effort, the Wikimedia Foundation is a team of just 157 committed employees who keep it all running behind the scenes. Hosting the fifth most popular site on the Internet isn't cheap, and online donations are the foundation's biggest source of income, so choosing the right combination of words to drive donations is a task that Chief Revenue Officer Zack Exley takes seriously. To brainstorm ideas for new banner appeals, the team will go to the park, a nearby bar or coffee shop, or their absolute favorite spot: San Francisco restaurant Eddie Rickenbacker's. Why does the Wikimedia team love Eddie Rickenbacker's so much? Because they have paper tablecloths.

Armed with pens, pencils, and crayons, the small team would venture down the block to Eddie's for a brainstorming session. By the end of the session, their tablecloth would be covered with words, phrases, and sentences. "They got used to us pushing the plates and stuff off and taking the whole tablecloth back to our office and putting it up on the wall," recalls Exley.

For a big fundraising push, Wikipedia's team comes up with dozens of variations to test. Finding the most effective words among the essentially endless options is a huge task—one that takes a lot of creativity and a lot testing. "You have to have a rule that if anybody feels strongly about testing something, you test it," Exley says.

There's one test in particular that stands out in Exley's mind.

There was a fundraising appeal that had done well as part of the site's landing pages: "If everyone reading this donated $5, we would only have to fundraise for one day a year. Please donate to keep Wikipedia free." One of the Wikimedia team members suggested testing what would happen if they replaced the last third of their fundraising banner with this line, and Exley agreed to a test (Figure 5.2).

This variation was a bit of a gambit, because setting the bar so distinctly at $5 had the potential to "anchor" users' minds at a lower level than the one suggesting "$5, $20, $50, or whatever you can." On the other hand, the logic of the appeal—and perhaps the very absence of higher dollar values—might persuade more users to give.

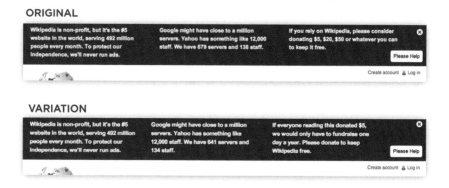

FIGURE 5.2 Original Wikipedia fundraising banner versus the "five dollars" banner variation.

The outcome: even though the five-dollar appeal lowered the average donation amount by 29 percent, the *rate* of donation went up by a whopping 80 percent, resulting in a net increase in overall amount raised of 28 percent.

Why versus *How*: Formstack

Deciding what to include in a site's main navigation, and how to arrange it, is key to establishing the flow of traffic and the focus of the site—and it can provoke strong differences of opinion. While redesigning their site, the team at online form builder Formstack sat around a table, considering their navigation. They all agreed on highlighting the form types, features, examples, and pricing, but were not sure what would be the best page to use as a lead.

The team settled on using *Why Use Us* as the lead navigation item because they suspected it would help persuade visitors that Formstack is a better choice than the competition. As analytics on the new site design filtered in, they noticed that visitors weren't clicking on "Why Use Us" as much as they had expected. That prompted a follow-up test: they tested whether naming the page *How It Works* would prompt more visits (Figure 5.3).

Although "Why Use Us?" was the question the Formstack team ultimately wanted to answer for their visitors, they decided to try the header "How It Works" because, their thinking went, it would invite visitors to investigate on their own without the obvious self-promotion. "How It Works" also helps a user unfamiliar with web form builders get his or her bearings on what it is that Formstack does as a company, whereas "Why Use Us" might suggest an explanation of how Formstack *differs* from its competitors, rather than what its product does in the first place.

FIGURE 5.3 Original Formstack navigation, "Why Use Us," versus variation, "How It Works."

In an A/B test pitting "Why Use Us" against "How It Works," the winner was clear. Naming the lead navigation item "How It Works" increased traffic to that page by nearly 50 percent, and also lifted two-week free-trial signups by 8 percent.

"Instead of getting bogged down in disagreements, we moved forward," says Jeff Blettner, a web designer at Formstack. "We knew that we would be able to come back after launch and test our hypotheses."

Nouns versus Verbs: LiveChat

LiveChat sells software that allows businesses to talk with their website visitors in real time. In order to figure out how to maximize the company's product sales, LiveChat visual designer Lucy Frank evaluated the steps most people take in signing up for the service. She found that most visitors sign up for a free trial before becoming paying customers, and so she hypothesized that increasing the number of people in free trials might result in more sales downstream.

Since the first step to starting a free trial is clicking the big shiny button on the homepage, Frank began her experimentation there. She decided to simply change the call-to-action text on the button from "Free Trial" to "Try it free," and see which version enticed more users to register (Figure 5.4).

The team hadn't expected to see much of a variation in terms of results from making such seemingly small changes. Yet the difference of just two words increased click-through rate by 14.6 percent.

This experiment is a great example of what we've seen again and again across a wide range of businesses. We usually give folks some pretty straightforward advice when they ask about how to improve their calls to action: *verbs over nouns*. In other words, *if you want somebody to do something, tell them to do it*.

Framing Effects

There are endless possibilities for any call to action, and it's not feasible to test them all. So, how do you focus your tests on only the possible alternatives that are most likely to have an impact? Having a good hypothesis of why a change will be effective is a crucial step, and one powerful theory to help you formulate it is called *framing*.

ORIGINAL

VARIATION

FIGURE 5.4 Original LiveChat call-to-action "Free Trial," versus variation, "Try it free."

Framing is the simple idea that different ways of presenting the same information will evoke different emotional reactions, and thus influence a person's decision. For example, as Nobel laureate psychologist Daniel Kahneman notes in *Thinking, Fast and Slow*:

The statement that "the odds of survival one month after surgery are 90%" is more reassuring than the equivalent statement that "mortality within one month of surgery is 10%." Similarly, cold cuts described as "90% fat-free" are more attractive than when they are described as "10% fat."[1]

Framing an idea in order to produce a desired emotional outcome in your reader has tons of applications, many of which fall outside of a traditional sales pitch. Any organization working to spur people to action, volunteer for a cause, sign a petition, donate money, and so forth, can make use of this technique to great effect.

A famous 1995 study by psychologist Sara Banks et al.[2] involved showing two groups of women videos on breast cancer and mammography in an attempt to convince them to get screened. The first group's video focused on *gains*, that is, it espoused the benefits of having a mammogram. The second group's video was *loss*-framed: it emphasized the risks of *not* having one. Though the two videos presented the same information, only 51.5 percent of those who saw the gain-framed video got a mammogram in the next year, whereas 61.2 percent of those who saw the loss-framed video did so.

There are no one-size-fits-all rules about message framing, and it's still important to test variations. However, an awareness of framing helps to define the scope of possibilities. You might, for instance, choose to avoid testing more equivalent phrases and

---

[1] Daniel Kahneman, *Thinking, Fast and Slow*, (New York, NY: Farrar, Straus and Giroux, 2011).
[2] Sara M. Banks, et al. "The effects of message framing on mammography utilization." *Health Psychology* 14.2, 178–184 (1995).

consider strikingly different ways you can frame your value proposition and test each of them. Try asking yourself:

- Is the language *negative* or *positive?* Do you, for instance, advertise what a product *has* or what it *doesn't* have?
- Is the language *loss-framed* or *gain-framed* (e.g., the mammography study)?
- Is the language *passive* or *action-oriented* (e.g., LiveChat's "Try it free" button)?

TL;DR

- There are endless word combinations to use on your website. Don't be afraid to **brainstorm and think broadly**: a testing platform **lowers the "barrier to entry"** of ideas, minimizes the risks of failure, and enables quick and potentially huge wins.
- Decisions around messaging and verbiage can easily lead to contentious debates on a team. A/B testing is a way to **put opinions aside** and get concrete feedback on what works and what doesn't. (We'll revisit this idea in Chapter 8.)
- If you want someone to do something, **tell them to do it**.
- Different ways of **framing** the same message can cause people to think of it in different ways. Play with alternative ways of framing the same information and see what differences emerge.

6

Fail Fast and Learn

Learning to Embrace the Times When A Beats B

If you want to increase your success rate, double your failure rate.

Thomas J. Watson, Former Chairman and CEO of IBM

After what we have been showing you, it may be tempting to think that *every* experiment you run will have a positive outcome. (Why, then, even run the experiment? Just keep changing the thing that you were going to test, and it'll be great!) The reality, of course, is that not every variation is going to beat the control.

Even "failed" experiments have their silver linings, however: recognizing that a particular change will harm your goals is inarguably better than simply making that change, and as an added benefit experiments like this are often the ones that teach us the most about our visitors and what drives them. Indeed, experiments that fail tend to contradict some assumption held by the tester, and the results can point to reasons why that assumption is wrong.

Prime Real Estate versus Familiar Real Estate: IGN

Gaming website IGN wanted to encourage more visitors to the video site that brings them a big portion of their ad revenue. So they tried running an A/B test where they moved the "Videos" link over to the left of the main navigation (Figure 6.1).

FIGURE 6.1 Original IGN navigation versus variation with repositioned "Videos" button.

There are plenty of organizations in which a change like this would have come down the chain of command once-and-for-all from the HiPPO—the Highest Paid Person's Opinion. But before making the change for good, IGN ran an experiment to see *exactly* how much of an increase they could expect to see from giving the "Video" link top billing.

Not only did the test, shockingly, show no *increase* at all, it showed that the new banner *dramatically reduced* the video click rate by 92.3 percent. If they had blindly moved the "Videos" link without testing it first, the change could have been disastrous. Because IGN gets so much traffic, it only took them a matter of hours to get statistically significant results. They were able to cease the experiment, return to the original design, and go back to the data for more answers.

The test saved IGN from a potential catastrophe that would have occurred had they simply rolled out the new navigation, but there's a bigger lesson. One of the biggest reasons for dramatic results like this one is that a lot of a site's traffic typically comes from *returning* visitors, users who are accustomed to seeing the site in a certain way—in this case, with the "Videos" link on the far-right side, not the far-left. When it's missing from the spot they normally go to find it, they're not going to do the work to locate it. Considering the root cause of the results offers lessons not only about proposed changes but, at a deeper level, about the testing *process* as well. Moving forward, the team can consider the fact that new and returning users are going to have very different experiences of the site. Keeping this in mind will bear fruit in subsequent tests. (We take a deeper look at the insights to be gained from traffic segmentation in Chapter 13.)

What's Good at One Scale Isn't Always Good at Another: E-Commerce

A/B testing is very prominent among e-commerce businesses. Many of those we've worked with are constantly testing something on their sites. As they say, "There's always something to be improved on or optimized."

Many retailers have customer reviews and star ratings displayed on their sites. One large online retailer discovered through testing that displaying the rating prominently on *individual* product pages helped conversion. So the e-commerce team there experimented with adding the ratings to the category page— the page one level up from the product page that shows all of the items in a category. It seemed like common sense to the e-commerce team: showing the stars on the spill page should motivate people to click through and view the products more often thereby increasing conversions. (Figure 6.2.)

Good thing they tested it because that was not the case, the variation did more harm than good. As it happened, showing

ORIGINAL

VARIATION

Nespresso® Citiz Red Espresso Machine
$249.95

★★★★★
Eligible for Free Shipping

Nespresso® Citiz Red Espresso Machine
$249.95

Eligible for Free Shipping

FIGURE 6.2   The original category product description with star ratings versus a variation without.

star reviews made customers convert 10 percent less. The test illustrates that *what works at one level of scale doesn't always work at another level*; what was good for the product page ended up being bad for the category page. It's a good reminder that just because something makes sense on a particular part of your site—or is even *proved* to be advantageous—doesn't mean you should roll it out to other parts of the site without checking first.

What Buyers Want Isn't Always What Sellers Want: Etsy

Handmade- and vintage-goods marketplace Etsy has over 42 million unique visitors per month and is among the Alexa Top 200 websites. A/B testing is an important means for the product developers and engineers to collect behavioral data about how Etsy's 800,000 sellers and 20 million members use the site.

Etsy users are shown an activity feed in which they can see highlights from fellow Etsy members they follow: the items those

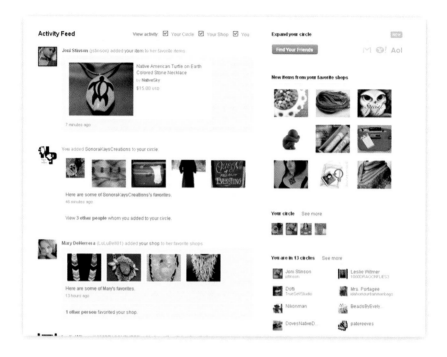

FIGURE 6.3   Original Etsy activity feed.

people are favoriting and purchasing. There are thousands of items posted to Etsy weekly, and this activity feed is a handy way for users to discover new items on the site (Figure 6.3).

The activity feed displays a combination of activities happening for buyers and sellers in one list. In what the team thought would be a much improved experience, they redesigned the feed and removed the "Your Shop" view from it, leaving only the "People You Follow" view. They A/B tested the original feed against the redesigned one to see how the redesign fared with users.

To the team's surprise, engagement with the feed dramatically decreased in the variation. After a closer look at the data, they discovered a certain type of use case that the team didn't anticipate. It turned out that sellers were using their own activity feed to manage their shops: as a timeline of what items they had listed at what times. The team envisioned the feed as a tool for buyers to scroll through what people were doing on the site. But *sellers* had been using this to manage their shops and the new "reskinning" removed this functionality for them.

Without this surprise result, the Etsy team would never have known about this use case. Now, not only could they take it into account during the redesign, they could actually *design for it.*

Their next iteration included two buttons: one called "Following," and another for "Your Shop" (Figure 6.4). The story ends happily with Etsy now actively building site functionality around a usage that, until their original redesign hit a snag, they had never known about.

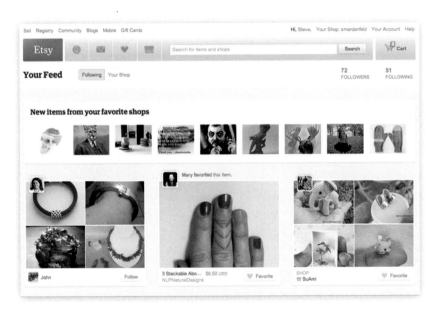

FIGURE 6.4   Final Etsy activity feed.

When a Win Isn't a Win (Is a Win): Chrome Industries

The Chrome e-commerce team has experimented with a plethora of image treatments for their urban biking products over the years, and recently decided to test whether a product *video* spurred more visitors to make purchases than did a static image (Figure 6.5).

ORIGINAL

VARIATION

FIGURE 6.5 Original Truk shoe screenshot with static image versus variation Truk shoe screenshot with video.

The objective of the test was to determine whether to commit more resources toward video development. The team picked one product to experiment with: their Truk shoe.

They measured the percentage of visitors to the Truk product page from the category page, the percentage of visitors who continued to checkout, and percentage of visitors who successfully ordered. After letting the test run for just under three months, the results were something of a wash. Users visited the Truk product page 0.5 percent more with the image, continued to checkout 0.3 percent more with the video, and successfully ordered 0.2 percent more with the video.

If anything, the video slightly edged out the static image, but because producing video involves a much higher investment from Chrome than the images, the verdict is actually a clear vote *against* the added production cost.

Chrome can table the issue for the time being, or it can further investigate the reason why video didn't convert, rather than moving forward under the assumption that video will drive sales and ramping up a full-blown video asset initiative that won't necessarily prove its return on investment. If the team does choose to test video down the line (e.g., in seeing how lifestyle-oriented video might compare against product-oriented video), they can at least be confident that there's little risk in running the follow-up test, since they've proven that video won't hurt conversion. They may also decide simply to allocate their energies elsewhere and experiment with optimizing different portions of the site entirely, where there may be bigger unrealized gains awaiting.

TL;DR

- What works for **returning users** may not work for new users, and vice-versa.
- **Something that works on one page may not work on another**; something that works at one scale may not work at another.
- What one type of user wants may not be what another type of user wants. A failed test, sometimes more than a successful test, may prompt a drill-down that reveals a **key difference between segments of users**.
- Sometimes a variation may win against the original, but it may not **win by enough of a margin** to justify the implementation overhead or other drawbacks of the variation that are external to the test itself.
- Any test that reveals that an initiative isn't performing is a blessing in disguise: it allows you to **free up resources** from things that aren't working and divert them to the things that are.

Implementing A/B Testing: Play-by-Play Guide

You've seen what A/B testing can do, and you've explored some of the key principles for getting the most out of A/B testing in your own business. There's one final principle: *start today*. Where Part I of the text focused on *what* to test, Part II discusses *how* to implement testing within the framework of your organization. Although it seems like a simple concept, we know it can sound a bit daunting, so we provide you with all the information you need. Let's go.

Choose the Solution That's Right for Your Organization

Deciding Whether to Build, Buy, or Hire

W e've explored some case studies that illuminate A/B testing's guiding principles and high-level concepts. Now it's time to get started, and that means it's time to get *practical*.

The first step is making a high-level decision about how you'll bring testing onboard: you can *build* your own testing tool in-house, *buy* a testing platform, or *hire* a consultant or agency to do the testing for you. There's no wrong choice, and each has its pros and cons. Indeed, many organizations elect to combine more than one of these approaches. We walk you through the things to consider when making the decision about what's best for your needs.

Option One: Build

Building a testing solution in-house is a viable option for organizations that have significant engineering resources available. We've found that most companies don't decide to suddenly build a testing tool from scratch without an engineering team that's closely tied to the process. A homegrown testing tool is usually something that organizations add on to an already established data-gathering and analytics machine.

Building an in-house solution requires substantial engineering effort, so it's rare for small companies with limited engineering resources to pursue this path. Typically only larger teams with specialized needs and enough dedicated engineering resources to pull it off will build a solution for themselves. For example,

Amazon has invested considerable effort over many years to build an extensive testing platform that is integrated closely with their website, product catalogue, and customer database.

There are many reasons why a company might choose to invest in a homegrown testing tool, but the biggest is probably the desire to run experiments that require a deep connection with proprietary internal systems, like Amazon's customer database in the example above. Custom-built testing platforms can provide specialized experiment targeting capabilities, tight integration with your build/deploy systems, and the ability to experiment with complex, server-side logic, like a search ranking algorithm.

Sometimes the decision to build an A/B testing capability to the website arises out of iterative additions to an in-house analytics platform. This was the case for Etsy, an e-commerce site that sells handmade and vintage goods. Today, their team runs every change or new feature release through an A/B test, but they didn't always work that way.

Dan McKinley started at Etsy in 2007, and discusses how they didn't do any measuring or A/B testing in the early days. "Nor did I really have any conception that we *should* have been doing it," he confesses. By 2011, McKinley had noticed a pattern in the way they developed products. As he describes it, the engineers would spend a great deal of time and effort working on a new feature up front. They would release that feature, and then talk about it at a company-wide meeting where there would be a lot of applause for the new feature. Then they would move on. Two years later, they would eliminate the feature they had spent all their time and effort developing—because it turned out that nobody was using it.

"I realized that we were failing in what we were trying to do; we just weren't very good at realizing that we were failing,"

McKinley told us. "[We wanted] to be better at realizing we were failing, and if at all possible, not fail. And that was the motivating factor in my getting into experimentation on the web."

Etsy has had access to a lot of data, data engineer Steve Mardenfeld explains, pretty much since the site launched. In turn, they have tools to collect, examine, and analyze that data in an effort to improve the user experience on the site. For example, examining the data lets them improve their search algorithms and recommendations. Whenever the engineers created a new feature, they would release it to a small percentage of users and look for any operational concerns. Once they knew it was functioning well (i.e., it wouldn't break the site) they would release it to 100 percent of Etsy users.

"So we were already doing the basic idea of A/B testing; we just weren't actually measuring anything," Mardenfeld says. "It just seemed like a really good fit to try to shoehorn this into the process that we already had."

Etsy's team of 100+ engineers decided to go with an in-house testing tool because they already had the infrastructure in place to support A/B testing. All they had to do differently was start tracking how the new experience performed against the original experience.

The A/A Test

When building your own A/B testing tool from scratch, one of the obvious areas of concern will be simply making sure that the tool is functioning accurately. One of the handiest ways to verify the accuracy of a testing tool is an *A/A test*. An A/A test, as the name implies, involves testing two *identical* versions of your page to ensure there are no statistically significant differences reported between them. If there are, then something fishy or erroneous may be happening with the way the test is being run or the way the data is collected or analyzed. An A/A test is a good way to assure yourself (and your boss) that your testing platform is functioning correctly.

Option Two: Buy

Let's talk about what you get when you buy a testing platform. Most follow the *Software-as-a-Service (SaaS)* model; in other words, you won't download anything or purchase a physical product. Rather, integration happens as easily as a one-time copy-and-paste onto your site, after which you access the software through the web and your tests and data live in the cloud. Buying a testing platform makes sense for a range of group sizes—individuals, small companies, and large companies. At Optimizely we work with companies ranging from self-service startups to Fortune 100s that are equipped with large testing teams. SaaS solutions offer a number of advantages:

- *Built-in features:* An obvious advantage of buying a testing solution is that advanced testing features are included in your purchase. (You can, for example, target visitors from Facebook who see one variation, and compare them to Pinterest visitors who see a different one; there is more on targeting in Chapter 13.) Commercial testing software is typically purchased as a subscription and many platforms offer multiple subscription tiers, with additional built-in features available in higher tiers.
- *Automatic updates:* When building a homegrown testing platform, the ability to have total control over the platform

requires an ongoing engineering commitment: everything the company wants the testing suite to incorporate requires engineers to build, test, and maintain it over time. A company using an off-the-shelf SaaS product will effectively remain at the cutting edge without additional effort.

- *WYSIWYG editing:* Leading A/B testing SaaS platforms enable marketers, advertisers, designers, and other non-technical users to easily create and test page variations, using a visual what-you-see-is-what-you-get (WYSIWYG) editor that doesn't require writing any custom code.

- *Trustworthy reporting:* Accurate and reliable statistical reporting and calibration are essential for any data-driven organization. When you purchase an off-the-shelf testing solution, you're buying something teams have spent time building, optimizing, and debugging. You can therefore trust them to give you accurate results about how your tests performed. What's more, these platforms are constantly being tested by the thousands of clients using them. (If you want to test the tool's accuracy yourself, you can of course run an "A/A test" as discussed above.)

- *Professional Support:* Most A/B testing platforms offer some form of dedicated technical support, and some even offer additional consulting services (for an additional charge). Technical support is especially important for teams in which non-technical users are driving the testing process.

- *Community:* When you sign up for an A/B testing platform, you are joining an existing community of users who are available to answer questions, give technical support, and suggest best practices.

Questions to Consider When Evaluating an A/B Testing SaaS Solution

1. Does the platform *integrate with other tools* you already use? For most businesses, an A/B testing tool will complement the other tools you're already using, especially analytics. The more your efficiency, data collection, and lead-generation/nurture tools communicate with each other, the more effectively you can use them in concert. Plus, integrating all of these can maximize the ROI you get out of each service alone.

2. Does it *meet your budget?* Testing solutions charge in a variety of different ways and while we encourage the reader to explore her options, ultimately the decision should come down to ROI: will the gains achieved by regular testing outweigh the usage fees paid for the platform? If budget is a concern, it may be possible to start small and expand: for example, for companies with multiple web properties or an international presence it might make sense to start with a single property/region and expand as you begin to realize gains.

3. How well do you gel with the *platform provider's team* and *support approach?* Because many tools can provide similar features technologically, the brand's personality, dedication to customer success, and availability are other critical elements to consider. Support on the platform must come from the platform provider, so ensuring the help is there if you need it is important. It may indeed be the variable that helps make your decision, since what differentiates one testing tool from the next is, in large part, the people. Are you looking for a team of people that can come up with great testing ideas for

you? If you're new to A/B testing, you might need a company that has dedicated support resources available 24/7 should you have questions.

Option Three: Hire

The final option is to hire an agency or an optimization consultant to do testing for you. An agency is a service independent from the client that provides an outside point of view on how best to sell the client's products or services—or in this case, optimize the client's website. Most digital marketing agencies are quickly adding A/B testing to the list of services they offer; they're also partnering with testing platforms in order to use them on clients' websites. Companies can hire agencies or consultants as short- or long-term solutions for testing.

There are myriad reasons to outsource testing. For instance, a company that doesn't have the internal resources to allocate to testing will instead choose to hire another entity to take care of all strategy and testing implementation. In another scenario, a company might have the bandwidth for ideating tests but lack the technical know-how to execute them. In this case, they'd work with an agency to implement tests. The reverse is also common, that is, for a company to purchase a testing platform and work with a strategic consultant to come up with test ideas.

If you outsource any part of testing—either the creative or the actual execution—then there are a few things to look for before you sign a contract. You want to make sure that the third party has a good track record with optimization strategy and implementation. They should be experts in each testing platform they offer, and provide technical support should you need it. With many agencies you'll pay the agency per-hour or per-experiment, and some also offer "unlimited" or "constant" testing programs: for a fixed price they conduct an unlimited number of tests within an overall program. Compare plans and think about what will work best for your needs before signing on.

It comes down to a tradeoff between investing time and training in building a team internally, or investing money in an agency. If you're not ready to build an internal testing team who will use a homegrown platform or an SaaS, then your best option is to hire an outside service to handle your testing.

The Choice Is Yours (and Your Team's)

In essence, the choice between buying, building, or hiring a testing solution depends on what makes the most sense based on a variety of factors that only you and your team can assess.

As co-founders of an optimization SaaS, it's hard for us to stay *entirely* objective, but the truth is that everyone's needs will be different. It's up to you to consider your own situation and then decide which solution will work best.

The decision need not occur in a silo; in fact it behooves you to *anticipate pushback* from your team and invite them to be part of the decision-making process. In order for A/B testing to become a viable solution for your company, everyone needs to trust the data that comes out of a test. If a couple of people don't trust what the A/B testing platform proves to be true, the entire discussion will center around questioning the validity of the data rather than what the data means. If you have a usability or IT team, make sure you have their blessing before making a decision. Start cementing buy-in up the chain of command from the moment you start considering which solution works best for your organization. If everyone feels good about the tool you're using, then *actually testing* will be much easier.

Remember that people might see A/B testing as another step in an already long process, not to mention that it could be a completely new (and hopefully exciting) framework for how decisions are made. Nothing will scare people away faster than mandating they run every change to the website through an A/B test before rolling it out. No matter how shocking the data is or how sleek the testing tool looks, it won't work if the team is ambivalent toward it. Nothing can replace a person who is genuinely interested and curious about A/B testing. Unite the team around the fact that A/B testing is the most powerful way to turn clicks into customers *before* you select a path to get there.

The good news is that "all roads lead to Rome." No matter which route you choose, you'll be taking your first step on the road to a better website and a better user experience.

The next step, of course, is running your first test. And that's where we pick up in Chapter 8.

TL;DR

- Building your own testing platform requires a significant and ongoing engineering investment, but can ultimately provide the greatest level of control and the **tightest integration** with your team and deployment cycles.

- An **A/A test** is a helpful way to ensure that your solution is functioning, reporting, and analyzing correctly.

- Many A/B testing Software-as-a-Service (SaaS) platforms are easy to use **without requiring engineering support**: marketers and product people without a coding background can create and run variations in a visual WYSIWYG environment.

- An agency can help your team with the **ideation** of tests, **execution** of tests, or both.

- When picking the solution that best fits your company, consider making **key stakeholders** part of the exploration process. The earlier you bring others on board, the easier it will be to get buy-in.

8

The Cure for the HiPPO Syndrome

Getting Buy-In and Proving Value

There is a practical side to the success of A/B testing at your organization, and success depends not only on the tests themselves, but equally on the *adoption* of testing as a cultural practice in your organization.

The HiPPO Syndrome Has a Cure

Many companies, even in an increasingly data-driven market-place, still unfortunately succumb from time to time to what we call the "HiPPO Syndrome": allowing decisions to be made according to the Highest Paid Person's Opinion rather than the data. What this means for the would-be A/B testing hero is that sometimes you may find yourself encountering various forms of passive and/or active resistance to adopting a testing-driven methodology. Here are a few ways to start curing the HiPPO Syndrome at your own workplace, and to move your organization toward an openness and eagerness for experimentation and a willingness to take the numbers seriously even when they're most surprising:

> DAN: I learned an important lesson about experimentation during my first year working at Google, when my mentor explained how I could convince my boss's boss to let me try something. Even at a fairly data-driven company like Google it was hard to convince the higher-ups to do something potentially risky or radical, and it's always a challenge to

get people's support to launch a new product or create a new feature since there's always the concern that perhaps nobody will use it. The key phrase in receiving this higher-up's blessing, my mentor explained, was to say, "Let's just run an experiment." In that context, the idea became an irresistible investigation into whether it would be worth their time and money—not a hard-and-fast decision of whether to make a permanent change.

A/B testing neutralizes the ideological and replaces it with the empirical. Instead of, "I *feel* we should do X because that's what I feel," a culture of A/B testing encourages both curiosity and humility, where people say, "I hypothesize that X is better than what we have right now. I don't have the data today, but let's run an experiment and test it." After that process is complete, A/B testing then offers the much stronger claim: "I *know* we should do X because of the evidence that it's the right thing to do."

Many features and functions take longer to prioritize than they do to build. In the time you've fully debated whether to develop the feature, you could have already had someone implement it and gather data from an A/B test on how it works. With the data in hand, you can then make an informed, data-driven decision about how to move forward with the project.

There are two things we would say to anyone in a position of decision-making authority who might be fearful of giving up his or her HiPPO status in the face of a more data-driven culture: The first is simply that, ultimately, data-driven companies win because they've made listening to and understanding their customers a basic component in their decision-making process. You have a competitor somewhere doing the same thing you do—but in a more data-driven way. And they will beat you, because they're listening to the numbers.

The second is that eliminating the need for a HiPPO can be liberating for an organization because it eliminates the requirement that everyone involved in a decision be a know-it-all. When people feel comfortable saying "I don't know, but let's run an experiment," they're more inclined to take risks by trying things outside the norm. The value in each individual then derives not only from their ability to make decisions but also their ability to generate hypotheses, and these can come from all levels in your org.

Another benefit of a more data-driven culture: *fewer and shorter meetings*. Former Senior Product Marketing Manager Jarred Colli describes the cultural shift he witnessed at Rocket Lawyer since he and a colleague began their first A/B experiments:

> Where previously, people would argue over what kind of headlines you use or what kind of picture, and you would spend hours drilling down on some stupid detail, now we don't have those conversations anymore, since we'll test all that stuff. We'll figure out whatever is best.

"You have to take egos out of the equation," agrees Netflix Experimentation Platform Manager Bryan Gumm. "And the only way to do that is to be empirical."

Winning Over the Stakeholders

It's also important, particularly in large organizations, to understand which key stakeholders you need to win over throughout the organization. To do this, identify some experiments you can run that will give you early wins and allow you to make the case for a continued investment. You don't want the first test you run to be contentious with the people whose buy-in you're trying to win. It's critical that this initial test clearly prove value *without* pissing people off.

"What I really like to focus on are good tests, tests that you know are almost like slam-dunks or very quick wins," Scott Zakrajsek, Global Web Analytics Manager for Adidas, advises. "What that does is help you understand how the platform works and how to use it. You can identify it as a win, pat yourself on the back, communicate that to the organization, thank everybody involved, and get everybody on board with a success."

When starting out, it's just as important to know what *not* to do as what to do. One thing to avoid at the outset: running a really complex test that involves deep technical integrations. If it doesn't work, the stakeholders may lose patience with the testing platform, or with testing itself.

Whereas the homepage is frequently (and naturally) the first area of the site that comes to people's minds for optimization, this thought is worth reconsidering, especially if your organization holds the homepage sacred. It's typically a highly visible (thus highly scrutinized) part of the site; what's more, the homepage is typically far from the ultimate goal for which you're optimizing. We often recommend starting with a *product page*, for two reasons: it's less visible, and it's closer to checkout. Take some time to establish a clear case study here to prove to the folks who control the homepage that it's worth investing and continuing to expand.

"There used to be some kind of 'sacred cows,' that you can't mess with this, you can't change this," Jarred Colli explains. After Rocket Lawyer saw an approximately 50 percent improvement in the conversion rate over a year's worth of tests, that attitude changed completely: "Now," says Colli, "we'll try everything."

Leading human capital solutions provider CareerBuilder decided to give A/B testing a grand entrance within the company.

"When we came onboard, we actually brought several of the product owners in and had a daylong competition," explains Senior Internal Business Systems Analyst David Harris. They paired each product with a developer and had them spend a day coming up with ideas for tests to run on their respective parts of the site. It wasn't simply an exercise: the tests each team brainstormed went live within the day, and then the group reconvened the following day to see which teams saw overnight results and what those results looked like. It was important, Harris says, to impart not only a sense of familiarity but also a sense of ownership: "This isn't just a training. We are going to have you spend the rest of the day going in and applying this to your business, to your area of the business."

Communicate Findings and Value to Your Team

Communicating A/B testing's findings and value to the team, whether it be large or small, is an important part of month one—and every month. Consider weekly, monthly, or quarterly results-sharing meetings with key stakeholders. Let them know what you've been up to. It will help the organization, as well as your career, because you've *quantified your value* in a way that may be difficult for roles that don't use testing.

"Stakeholder support and buy-in only happens if you do a good job of communicating and sharing things that you are learning," explains Nazli Yuzak, Senior Digital Optimization Consultant at Dell. "Making sure that we are communicating our wins, communicating the learning, and sharing those large-level trends with the rest of the organization actually becomes an important part of the culture, because that's where we are able to showcase the value we bring to the organization."

You want to let others in on what you've learned from your first tests. You can't always predict who within the organization will turn out to be an evangelist for testing. We've seen companies handle this communication many different ways. Having built a testing culture at three large e-commerce sites—Staples, Victoria's Secret, and Adidas—Scott Zakrajsek suggests sending straightforward emails with subject lines like "A/B Test Completion," or "A/B Test Results." Include *screenshots* of the variations and results in those emails: images are likely to be more memorable than just the results alone, as they give a clear indication of the evolution of the site over its optimization—"where we were" versus "where we are now."

Evangelize and Galvanize: Lizzie Allen at IGN

It's one thing to get people excited about A/B testing; it's another thing entirely to encourage people to make it an integral part of their daily practice. This is what it takes, though: making the testing culture at your organization contagious.

This might seem like a daunting task. But if an entry-level data analyst can single-handedly turn a 15-year-old, 300-person company into a shining example of A/B testing prowess, you can do it, too.

When Lizzie Allen joined the gaming news site IGN as a data analyst in 2010, the company had never heard of A/B testing. Allen was astounded that such a prominent content website did not use this approach to test its assumptions, especially when making editorial decisions. So she took on the challenge of introducing the company to A/B testing, and helping to establish a culture where decisions would be rooted in data. "When you tweak any sort of process in a large organization, you have to throw your weight around. When you're entry-level, you don't have a lot of weight to throw around. I had to use some untraditional and somewhat ballsy methods in order to promote A/B testing," Allen says.

In month one, she introduced the company to testing through training sessions. She worked with folks on the editorial team to educate employees throughout IGN about the practice. These sessions specifically centered on the value of testing two different headlines to see which one garnered more clicks. When the early buzz and excitement started to dwindle, Allen perceived that people saw A/B testing as an extra step in an already established, already functioning process. "There wasn't a foundation of data-minded people to support it, and I needed to cultivate that," she says.

Her strategy, then, was to shock people—a lot of people—to prove why A/B testing was so vital to business. Allen *gamified* A/B testing by turning the site's tests into a competition. (IGN is a gaming site, after all.) The "A/B Master Cup" was born. Inspired by the website whichtestwon.com, Allen would once a week send out a test that IGN had run that week and ask people to choose which variation they thought had won. She used the company's internal chat tool (Yammer) to send out screenshots of the different variations. At the end of each month, she would crown the person who picked the most test winners correctly as the "A/B Master."

She found that, overwhelmingly, *everybody failed*. In fact, some months went without a winner at all, because people guessed wrong so often. The contest started a lot of conversations, and began to instill a sense of humility, and also of intrigue. One week at a time, Allen built a groundswell of data-driven thinkers who were curious and eager to "figure out the puzzle that is the Internet user base for a video game content publishing site."

When asked for advice for building a testing culture at a company, Allen puts it simply:

Be obnoxious. Question assumptions. Be that jerk in the back of the meeting who raises her hand and asks, "All right, so why are we doing this?" when everybody is going, "Fine." That sometimes stops people in their tracks. You do that enough, and [people] will actually prepare. [They'll start to] think about gathering metrics and data.

"You are probably going to be a little bit annoying," Allen says. But that's okay, because even though others might not be aware of it yet, you're changing things for the better. "Now, I walk through the halls and hear 'Oh, we should test this, we should test that,' she explains. "It's almost like I need a long couch in my area so people can sit back and talk about their hypotheses. That's the beautiful place that we're in."

TL;DR

- In some workplaces, and to varying degrees, the **HiPPO Syndrome** holds sway, but often all it takes are a few humble tests and a curiosity and interest in testing begin to take root.
- Allay the wary with the reassurance that you're not proposing sudden changes: it's **"just an experiment."**
- In month one, run a test that is politically palatable and easy enough that it can show a **quick win**. Product pages can be a great place to start.
- **Share wins** not only with your immediate boss but, if possible, with the company at large. Communication is key in getting people to care about testing.
- Get creative with how you **introduce stakeholders and co-workers** to A/B testing.

The A/B Testing Dream Team

Bringing Everyone Together

A/B testing is by its nature collaborative and interdisciplinary, straddling traditional departmental lines: marketing, product management, engineering, and design. As a result, the adoption and long-term success of testing requires thinking about how it will fit into your company, not just philosophically and culturally, but *organizationally*. In this chapter we'll explore several different approaches and look at how different organizations have worked testing into their organizations.

The Centralized Team

At every place Adidas's Scott Zakrajsek has worked, the testing team has started as a team of one or two.

> At Staples I was the only person and we basically had to hire up from there, so we hired a front-end web-developer who was just for testing. We hired a creative designer who was just for testing; we hired an additional two analysts.
>
> I think your key players are someone with a good project management background to manage the pipeline. Someone with attention to detail to be the coordinator and make sure you have all the right creative assets. You need a web-analytics person to read the results and do post-test segmentation. That said, smaller companies can do it well with teams of one person. The "beg-borrow-steal" method works well, too.

Zakrajsek currently runs the global analytics and optimization team for Adidas. His team handles all A/B testing responsibilities companywide, including executing tests and delivering results; if anyone has an idea for a test, they tell Zakrajsek, and his team knows what to do with it. The strategy over the longer term, however, is to make this team the centralized keeper of institutional testing knowledge while eventually *decentralizing* the test execution: entrusting product managers with responsibility of running tests for different areas of the site (which we'll discuss ahead).

The Decentralized Team

The alternative to a centralized structure, where there is a single testing team to whom all other departments come for testing ideas and/or execution, is a *decentralized* structure, where each product manager (PM) has autonomy, the responsibility for a different part of the website, and the authority for testing that set of pages.

CareerBuilder is another company that has moved in this direction. "Previously most of our testing had resided within our development area," explains Senior Internal Business Systems Analyst David Harris. "If one of the product owners were looking to experiment with something, they had to submit something down into our development group, who would make those changes and test them on their own, so [testing] was kind of siloed out by itself a little."

The adoption of a no-code-necessary A/B testing platform enabled a change. "Part of what we were eager to do was really to move that into the hands of people who had a more direct stake in that particular page or area, to be able to make those changes themselves and then bring a data-supported request to development as opposed to just submitting the test and waiting for the result."

Harris is the point person for all things A/B testing from an administrative standpoint: he trains every new tester on how to use the tool and best practices, and if people have quality assurance questions (like how long to run a test), he takes care of it. However, he is *not* part of the process whereby product owners decide what to test. And he explains why: "We want to give people room to have creativity and freedom to do what they're doing within those [product] areas."

A decentralized model allows for greater independence, and reduces the potential for an organizational bottleneck, as each team can be testing its own part of the site in parallel. However, the disadvantage in comparison to a centralized testing team is that these separate testers face the challenge of staying coordinated and in communication about their results and best practices.

At Netflix, A/B testing also happens at the product manager level: each PM operates testing and analytics for a specific streaming platform such as Xbox, web, or tablet.

Bryan Gumm is Manager of Experimentation for the PS3 and Wii consoles, and has worked on various other platforms in the past. "We change that up about every three to six months just so all of the analysts are well-versed in all areas of the product," he says.

Twice a week, the vice presidents of product and product managers meet for strategy meetings to review and analyze test results and vet ideas for future tests. "Every six to eight weeks, there's a Customer Science Meeting with our CEO and basically all of the C-levels and we present what we're testing, what has been rolled out, and what is testing and is not being rolled out because it didn't work," Gumm explains.

CareerBuilder has also focused on how to balance the autonomy of their different testing groups with the need for coordination among them, and part of their solution has involved the creation of internal distribution lists around testing. "We basically encourage anyone who is conducting a test to push out a communication to everyone that's within that distribution before they set it, or at the time they set it live," Harris explains.

In that communication, the tester includes screenshots of the original page and variations being tested and a short write-up of the test goal. When the test has reached a statistically significant conclusion, the tester sends a follow-up with results and the key takeaways. Communicating findings and best practices is especially important for the internal team when the test requires code to set up.

With testing teams in 47 different countries, Dell takes a similar approach to transparency into what's being tested and what's coming up. "You've got to make sure you have a process to bring everybody together," explains Dell Marketing Director Ed Wu. "We have a meeting every two weeks with all the global and regional stakeholders and we say, 'Guys, here's the goal we have over the next cycle, here's the test idea we have,' and they can all lock in on the same test idea."

The Three Key Ingredients of a Scalable Testing Strategy

At Optimizely we've worked with companies of every size who are establishing testing teams, and over the years we've noticed that the most successful teams included four key elements:

1. A point person

    What we have heard again and again from the companies we've worked with is that no matter how large or small the team of people executing A/B tests is, at least one person has to live, breathe, and evangelize optimization. The first step is to give someone ownership of testing. This individual might have other jobs besides A/B testing: Lizzie Allen, for instance, held this role alongside her other data-analyst duties at IGN.

If no one at your company is willing to take on the responsibilities, we encourage you to invest in hiring someone who can dedicate themselves to A/B testing. While you know by this point that A/B testing is tremendously valuable, it's easy to neglect it in favor of more "urgent" tasks. There's usually a blog post, a product release, or a code review that can take precedence. In reality, in terms of the bang for the buck, A/B testing is one of the best possible investments of an organization's resources because it makes every dollar spent on other marketing activities more effective. Without clear direction on who will *own* A/B testing, however, you risk its becoming another item on the to-do list. To ensure that it gets done, make it part of a job description.

2. Advocates across your organization

Your A/B testing point person (or team) won't be effective in isolation. They'll need allies across your marketing department and your engineering and product teams to be successful. This is not only because of the help they can provide in generating hypotheses and implementing experiments, but also because they're key in ensuring that testing is a regular part of the product/marketing/design planning process.

As Wu explains, allies are pivotal to growing a testing culture:

> At Dell we have global stakeholders, the teams responsible for longer testing programs, and we also have

regional stakeholders that are responsible for day-to-day, weekly, monthly revenue generation, lead generation, etc. Most of [the regional stakeholders] have become believers of A/B testing and analytics. They have become champions for us. The testing teams ourselves, we are basically the carpenters—we founded our program and over time [the regional stakeholders] have become strong believers of ours so we can continue to fund the growth of our program.

3. Enabled testers

Empowering and enabling the people in charge of running the tests is one of the most important components of building a testing culture. The most successful customers we work with are the teams who allow people to test with creativity and resources.

What do we mean by this? Testing cannot work without *creativity*, that is, thinking outside of what exists on your site today and having the willingness to test it. Successful testing also requires certain *resources*: training, design/engineering work, educational tools, best practice information, and institutional encouragement. It's vital to create an environment where the people doing testing feel enabled and have the resources they need for the team to reach its full potential.

4. A track record

As the volume and impact of your tests increases, so does the need to keep track of what you're testing. First, come up with a *naming convention* for your tests. We recommend using *initials* when naming tests: a lone tester today may be part of a bigger team in a year, and so it's important to know who ran the test. You need to establish accountability and transparency early on.

Once you have a naming convention for your tests, start a log of tests run with their results: what worked, what didn't work, and why. As your company (or testing team) grows, it becomes crucial to educate new people on the past lessons. It's also extremely wise to have a record that will persist even if the tester leaves the company or role. It's dangerous to trust one person within an entire organization to keep this testing history in his or her head: if that person leaves, you risk losing all of those pieces of wisdom. Keep a shared document or internal wiki of your tests and include *screen-shots*. It will be a treasure trove to you.

Finally, if you run a test that requires a particularly complex or nuanced technical integration, use the log to record how you did it. Teams down the road may want to run a similar test, and you'll save them from having to reinvent the wheel.

TL;DR

- A/B testing is by nature **interdisciplinary** and **cross-departmental**. Collaboration is key.

- Some companies have a **centralized testing team** responsible for coordinating and executing all A/B tests companywide.

- Other organizations adopt a **decentralized** model, where each product owner/manager is responsible for testing within his or her product domain.

- Regardless of which structure you adopt, make sure there is at least one **point person** within the organization whom people can come to about all things testing.

- Ensure your point person or team maintains **allies across your organization** to ensure that testing is part of your planning process.

- Make sure that your testers are enabled and **empowered to be creative**, and that the friction of running and iterating new tests is low.

- **Maintain records** about who tested what and when, how the test was set up, and what the result was. This will enable your organization to work collaboratively to build up a set of collective wisdom and best practices.

10

Iterate, Iterate, Iterate

The Art of Asking Many Small Questions Rather than One Big One

When test results first start to come in, it's important to recognize that they're likely going to generate more questions than answers. These questions will likely also point to more assumptions you find you want to test. That's okay; in fact, that's how it's *supposed* to work. And that's the perfect starting point for your tests to come.

One of the biggest questions that we had when starting Optimizely was whether people would continue experimenting after they found a "local maximum," that is, the best set of tweaks for their current design or current funnel. We worried that people would spend a few months optimizing a site—a better headline here, different image there—and be done with it. We didn't want businesses to think of A/B testing as a finite, onetime process, and we acknowledged the disconcerting possibility that businesses would feel satisfied if the site worked better than before, and might throw in the towel and declare, "Well, enough of that! We're all done A/B testing."

Much to our delight, we've found that the opposite has occurred. After a few big wins, most people realize that they're just beginning the testing journey—and the success they've enjoyed propels them to keep going.

In month one, you run a couple of tests; you get some wins and you're adding those wins into the production code. Those wins might have been scattered around different pages of your site, since you've likely gone after the low-hanging fruit on various sections of the site. Hopping around like this is great for quick wins that prove value early on. However, you want to spend the next couple of months concentrating your optimization efforts on a specific area or areas of your site. This approach leads to richer, more valuable test results. It's absolutely fine to use the first month to test a product detail page one day, a landing page another day, and the "About" page the next. But over the next couple months, you want to pick *one* of those pages and focus a series of tests on it. Testing in a series, or *iterative testing*, is the goal here.

Multivariate Testing and Iterative Testing

It's possible to create large-scale tests to assess a number of different variables simultaneously, and these big, compound experiments are known as *multivariate tests*. For instance, two different button colors, three different calls to action, and five different images could all be tested at once, making for a total of $2 \times 3 \times 5 = 30$ different page combinations being shown to different users!

You may recall the example that began this book, from the Obama 2008 campaign: the campaign team used a multivariate test to optimize the best button and best media simultaneously, testing every combination of buttons and media.

One of the questions that we hear frequently is, "When should we use multivariate tests, and when should we use a sequence of single-variable tests?" It turns out this is actually a very nuanced question.

Among the most important things that multivariate tests enable you to discover are *interaction effects* between the different variables or elements you're testing. It might be possible, for instance, that image X performs worse than your control, and so does button Y—yet when X and Y are shown *together* they are significantly superior to the control.

It's a fear of these interaction effects that causes many people initially to assume that *everything* they want to test should be run as one massive multivariate experiment. We think that these fears are often misguided. Here's why.

For one thing, interaction effects do exist, but in *practice* they're relatively rare. Note that the button that performed best in the Obama 2008 multivariate test was also the button that performed best overall *without* taking the media into account. Likewise, the media that performed the best in the multivariate experiment was also the media that performed best overall without taking the button into account. The big multivariate test confirmed that these two indeed worked well together: there weren't any interaction effects that might have complicated those single-variable results.

Even if interaction effects are rare, why not just use multivariate tests for everything, just to be sure? The fact is that multivariate tests require *much more traffic* to produce statistically significant results for each combination. By multiplying the number of permutations, you're also multiplying the number of users that will need to go through your experiment, and the time you'll need to let the experiment run before you get your answer.

Having worked with thousands of customers in a wide variety of industries, we've found that the people who use website optimization most effectively run a series of simple A/B tests, and then incorporate the winner as they go along. They run four or five variations, figure out what works, incorporate that element, and then move on to the next test. When you judge the risk of interaction effects to be low, we strongly recommend that you *test nimbly*: start with simple independent A/B tests and *iterate* instead of trying to sort out everything all at once in a multivariate experiment.

"[Testing] gives us humility," says Principal Engineer Dan McKinley at Etsy. "It changes the way we build things." He explains, "There has been a dramatic change in the way we try to build products between 2007 and now, in that now . . . we are going to get there through smaller releases of things that we measure. We are not going to try to do 11 things at once. We'll if possible do 11 things in sequence."

There Are No Universal Truths: Always Be Testing

The world is a very big place; different websites and different products appeal to different people. One of the reasons why A/B testing is so important is that there are *no universal truths* when it comes to design and user experience. If universal truths existed, then A/B testing wouldn't: you'd just look at the rulebook. But because no two audiences are the same—and people are coming from an array of places and perspectives—it's crucial to understand and optimize the experimentation process.

More and more businesses have done so. It's typical to see companies running a number of tests at any time, relative to the time of year, product launches or various campaigns.

What does a long-term A/B testing strategy look like? As Senior Product Marketing Manager Jarred Colli, who led A/B testing for Rocket Lawyer, puts it: "Shifting the discussion from 'What's testable?' to 'Everything is testable.'"

Adopting the mantra "Always Be Testing" is one of the tenets of taking your testing program long-term.

Redesigning Your Redesign: CareerBuilder and the Optimizely Website

One of the mistakes we have seen companies make is undertaking a complete redesign of their site and *then* optimizing the new site using A/B testing. This is a violation of two core principles of A/B testing: *define success metrics* and *explore before you refine*.

The failure to define success metrics comes as a result of redesigning the site *without a goal*. Other than wanting to look more current, what are the specific targetable behaviors or actions you want the redesigned site to encourage in your users?

The failure to explore before they refine comes when companies pass up their biggest opportunity to get hugely meaningful data from their redesign: testing the new design itself. Instead of comparing the new page against a tweaked version of itself, test it against the old site. The bigger the change you're making, the more you want to be sure that it's having a positive effect. *Then* you can worry about refining from there, once you've rolled out the new design with *evidence* that it's doing a better job than the old one in the critical areas.

David Harris, Senior Internal Business Systems Analyst at CareerBuilder, talks about how the long-term adoption of A/B testing at CareerBuilder has involved what he calls "pulling testing ever farther up in the process": moving it from deployment to design. "It is during the very early stages of redesigning a page that we are incorporating in plans to test things—how we want to test them, what we want to test for, what conversions are important."

During the summer of 2012, we at Optimizely were planning a total website redesign. We felt there was an opportunity for us to hone our look and our message for new visitors. What better way to improve our own website than to eat our own dog food? We ran Optimizely on Optimizely.

Our previous site design made a clear and simple statement about our initial offering, an easy-to-use product for website A/B testing which we captured with our tagline: "A/B Testing You'll Actually Use." We discussed the opportunity we had to re-imagine a design that would maintain our core message and brand while providing additional benefits to visitors to our home-page and more broadly capture the value of A/B testing.

One other area of focus with the new site was providing a more comprehensive approach to engaging different visitor types. We have continued to learn over time how different customer types use Optimizely to achieve a wide range of different goals. To address this, we built out a series of pages that focused on the benefits of using Optimizely for each of these groups: agencies, developers, e-commerce sites, large "enterprise" sites, publishers, and small businesses.

Applying the approach of refine, explore, refine, our design team took to developing several concepts that could possibly achieve a new look and feel that could take our site experience to the next level in several areas. Ultimately, we agreed that the most important thing a potential tester can do on our site is enter a URL and experience our WYSIWYG editor firsthand. We focused our design efforts and our testing success metrics around maximizing the number of users who used our editor, and who signed up for an account. In addition to the key macro-conversion goals, it's important to track a wide range of goals to get a holistic sense of how the new site design performs.

In just about every metric we measured, the new site was a clear winner against the old one. After running the test on new visitors for just over a month, we were confidently able to declare a winner and push the new site live to all visitors. Most of our thoughts about what our original site lacked were proven true (Figures 10.1 through 10.8).

With a new design live, we can dive into a range of new tests already lined up as we refine from here. There is still plenty of great work to be done.

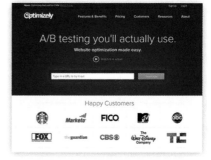

FIGURE 10.1 Original Optimizely homepage versus redesigned homepage.

FIGURE 10.2 Original Optimizely About page versus redesigned About page.

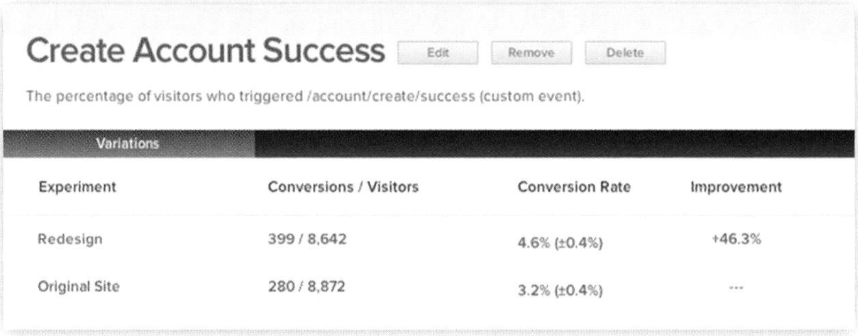

FIGURE 10.3 Create Account Success: Percentage of visitors who completed the "create an account" signup form.

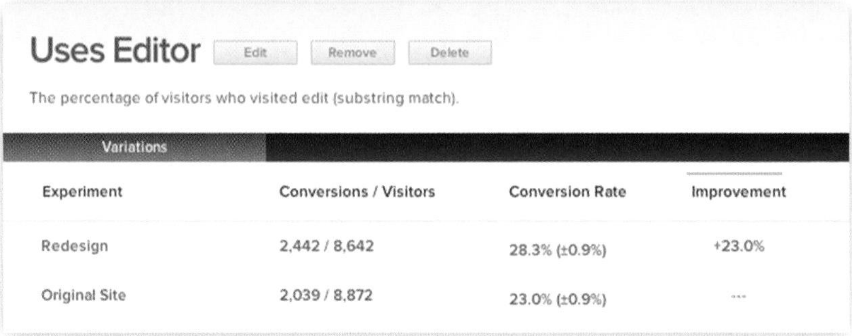

FIGURE 10.4 Uses Editor: percentage of visitors who entered a URL on the homepage and used the Optimizely editor.

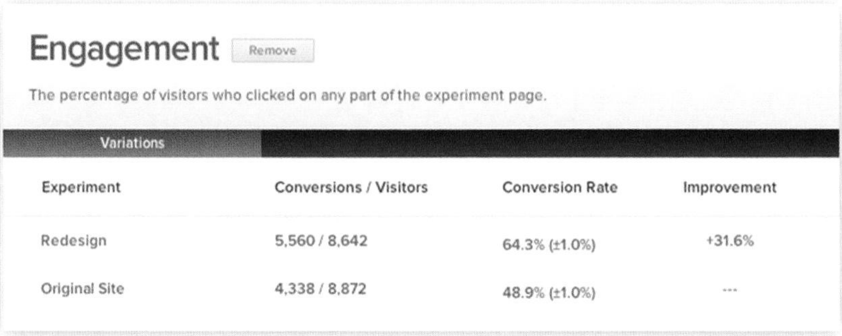

FIGURE 10.5 Engagement: this goal is included in every experiment created with Optimizely by default. It measures the percentage of visitors who click anywhere on the experiment page.

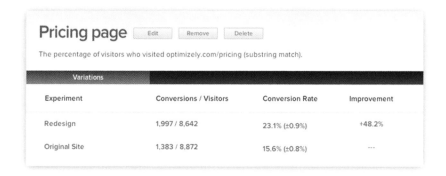

FIGURE 10.6 Visits Pricing: percentage of visitors who visited the Optimizely Pricing page.

Create Account Dialog Shown [Edit] [Remove] [Delete]

The percentage of visitors who triggered /account/create/show (custom event).

Variations			
Experiment	Conversions / Visitors	Conversion Rate	Improvement
Redesign	525 / 8,642	6.1% (±0.5%)	+30.2%
Original Site	414 / 8,872	4.7% (±0.4%)	---

FIGURE 10.7 Create Account Dialog Shown: percentage of visitors who submitted the free trial signup form on the homepage.

Experiment Started Successfully [Edit] [Remove] [Delete]

The percentage of visitors who visited /experiment/start/success (simple match).

Variations			
Experiment	Conversions / Visitors	Conversion Rate	Improvement
Redesign	286 / 8,642	3.3% (±0.4%)	+27.7%
Original Site	230 / 8,872	2.6% (±0.3%)	---

FIGURE 10.8 Experiment Started Successfully: percentage of visitors who landed on the experiment creation success confirmation page.

TL;DR

- **Multivariate tests** are a powerful way to test a number of variables simultaneously, and can reveal **interaction effects** between them. However, they require more traffic and can be slower to achieve statistical significance.

- We have found that the companies that have had the greatest success with A/B testing favor a nimbler, more **iterative approach** that tests a handful of different variants of a single variable at a time and incorporates the winner as they go on to the next test.

- When working on a complex change like a site redesign, we recommend that you **move testing further up the process** so that it becomes something that happens *during* the design and rollout of the new site, rather than *after*.

Advanced Topics in A/B Testing

Having explored both the broad principles of A/B testing and the roadmap to implementing A/B testing within your own organization, it's time to go further. This final part of the text deals with a potpourri of advanced topics in A/B testing—including how testing can go awry, how to take testing beyond page design elements, and how to progress from giving your users the "average best" experience into something more personalized.

11

How A/B Tests Can Go Awry

Potential Mistakes and Pitfalls to Avoid

At this point in the book the hazards of *not* A/B testing should be clear; however, it's worth mentioning that A/B testing has its own set of pitfalls and "worst-practices."

Testing without Traffic

The good news is that you need only two things to conduct an A/B test: a website with some content on it, and visitors. The more traffic you have the faster you will see statistically significant results about how each variation performed.

What A/B testing your site *can't* do, however, is generate that traffic in the first place. A blogger who's just getting off the ground and has only 100 visitors per month would be better off focusing primarily on *content* and building a following of users (bolstered perhaps by SEO or paid ads) who provide traffic to the site *before* delving into the statistics of optimizing that traffic. After all, you have to generate the traffic in the first place before you do anything with it. (In addition, in a site's fledgling period, a handful of conversations with real users will offer more feedback than you will get from an A/B test on a sparsely trafficked site.) While optimization can help even the smallest enterprise, it's also true that testing becomes faster, more precise, and more profitable the more user traffic you have to work with.

The Beginning of the Funnel versus the End: UserVoice

Testing will occasionally reveal a change that increases one metric but decreases another. You'll recall from Chapter 2 that defining quantifiable success metrics is the first step in any test, and so it's worth reflecting on some nuances and complications around how to evaluate whether a test variation is in fact a "win."

The testing team at online help-desk software provider UserVoice hypothesized that removing fields from their free-trial signup form would increase the trial signup rate (Figure 11.1).

After the UserVoice team A/B tested the page, they found that, indeed, the fewer fields they required, the more people signed up for a free trial. However, they began to feel that perhaps

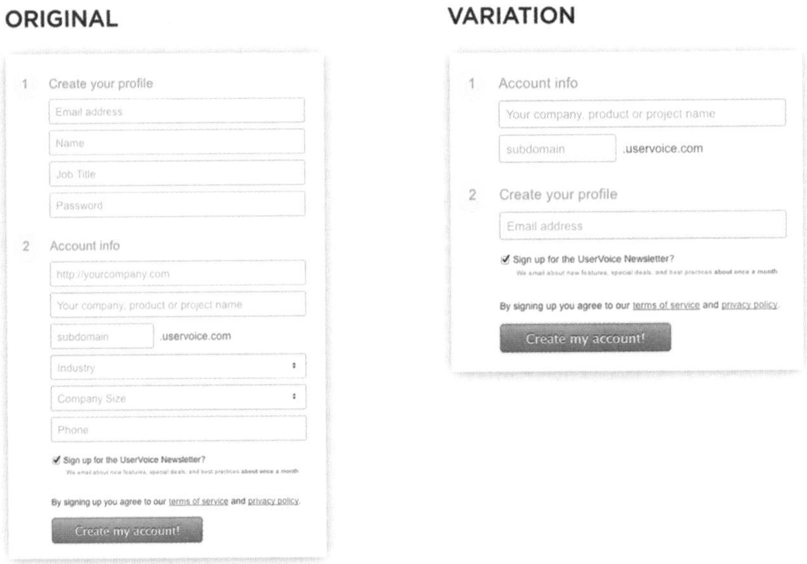

ORIGINAL

VARIATION

FIGURE 11.1 Original UserVoice signup form versus variation form with fields removed.

they'd made it *too* easy to run a trial. A plethora of people had begun trials, but the sales team was finding it increasingly difficult to determine who the best leads were.

The first thing they needed to do was decide what kind of leads they were going after. Were they seeking individuals who were well educated and informed about what UserVoice was and what it could offer them? Or did UserVoice plan to educate these people via email marketing *after* they became leads? Both scenarios are plausible and reasonable.

Here's where the *key performance indicators (KPIs)* began to clash. The marketing team was motivated to reach the broadest audience possible, while the sales team was motivated to turn the highest percentage of the most promising leads into customers. With the question of the free trial, it wasn't immediately clear which goal was best served in which way.

The UserVoice team began to notice that homing in on immediate metrics like the percentage of users that went from one page of their signup funnel to the next made it easy to get the wrong result from their A/B tests. "It's what I call *pushing failure down the funnel*," says co-founder and CEO Richard White. "We want quality leads, not quantity leads," he explains.

> Getting somebody to a page and getting somebody to use a product day-in and day-out are two different things. You end up with this insidious kind of race to the bottom, where you just want to remove all of the fields and everything and just say, "Go get your trial," and then they get into the trial and they have no idea why they're there.

> The goal will be a marketing site which should be educating them to get to the next step, so I think the tricky thing about A/B testing is the right variation may be the one where 80 percent of the people drop out on one page because they're

thinking this is not for them, but the other 20 percent of the people love it and sign up and try it.

Off-Brand Testing: Dell

There's a joke among A/B testing veterans that almost any variation of a button loses to a button that says, "Free Beer." But that doesn't mean that every company should liquidate its assets and go into the brewing business. More broadly, it's important that every company put its testing process into the broader context of its identity as a company.

Eric Ries, author of *The Lean Startup*, has witnessed many a cautionary tale, where a company's A/B test results have run it off the rails. "Abdicating product vision is a very common danger with A/B testing," says Ries. He recalls talking with an ex-employee of a company that went under. Ries asked the former employee what went wrong, and the employee explained, "Yeah, if you're on a social platform, and if all you do is A/B test all the time then you immediately get yourself into sexting, porn, and nasty stuff because that's what converts."

Not every company finds itself falling into quite such a dramatic identity crisis, but the broader point is one that almost any organization can relate to: how to balance customer feedback and brand identity. For example, an e-commerce site may find that displaying sale prices bigger and with big red strike-through lines improves their conversions. But that increase in conversions could cost them something potentially more valuable: their brand. The site may begin to look like a discounter when it's really a boutique. "It comes down to understanding who you are," says Chrome Industries e-commerce Director Kyle Duford. "Just because you can doesn't mean you should."

Many companies are extremely particular about their brand image to the point that they are not willing to test things that they wouldn't put live on their site.

It's sound advice. A question worth asking about every test is, "Would you be happy showing the winning variation to all of your traffic?" If not, then what exactly are you hoping to gain from the test?

There are several valid answers to this question, and it's worth pointing out that many companies do in fact experiment with things they wouldn't necessarily be committed to rolling out at full scale. One such company is Dell, where Marketing Director Ed Wu argues that there *can* be a place for testing variants of a page that the company isn't interested in implementing in the near-term.

Using A/B testing to learn about how visitors engage with certain types of content or color or messaging can be illuminating and can feed back into later conversations with Dell's brand team or the global site design team. "Our global design team has very consistent and very stringent guidelines in terms of what color you can use on dell.com," says Wu. The global guidelines for dell.com call for a blue banner of a specific hue at the bottom of the page, and Dell's testing team was interested in pushing back on that guideline to see whether that blue is in fact the best color to have on the site. So Wu's testing team worked with Dell's branding team and global design team to come up with some alternatives, including a bottom banner that was red. "[We] know that it's violating our brand standard, we would not be able to implement that, but eventually we'll all agree, let's go ahead and test it and understand how it works," says Wu. Testing for learning and understanding, not just conversions, allows Dell to "push the thinking" on what is optimal for the site.

TL;DR

- A/B testing can help even the smallest of organizations and sites, but it becomes more powerful the **more traffic** a site has. If your site is starved for traffic, A/B testing probably shouldn't be your first priority.

- Testing will occasionally reveal a change that increases one metric but decreases another. **Don't push failure down the funnel.**

- Consider whether you are willing to test a page variant that is in some way **off-brand** or one that you wouldn't necessarily be quick to roll out to all your users should it "win" the test.

Beyond the Page: Non-Website A/B Testing

How to Test Email and Pricing

U p to this point, we've primarily looked at examples where teams test a page's various design elements: forms, images, headlines, and layout. This chapter explores A/B testing beyond the page, in two different domains: email and pricing.

The *What* and the *When*: Prezi

Email is one of the most important things you can A/B test. Just as you can use A/B testing to make the elements of your website work better, you can A/B test emails to increase quantifiable success metrics like *open rate* and *click-through rate*. And just as you can roll out a website change gradually and gauge response before showing it to all users, it's easy and incredibly advantageous to roll out an email in the same way. First, select a portion of your total mailing list and send them a number of variations. Gauge your success metrics, and *then* send the email that works best to the remainder of your full list.

It was Halloween of 2011, and David Malpass—marketing analyst at cloud-based presentation tool Prezi—was planning to send out a huge email newsletter blast. He sent his boss, the director of marketing, three candidate subject lines:

1. "New Tricks & Treats"
2. "New features: Templates, Google Image Search"
3. "Create a beautiful Prezi in minutes"

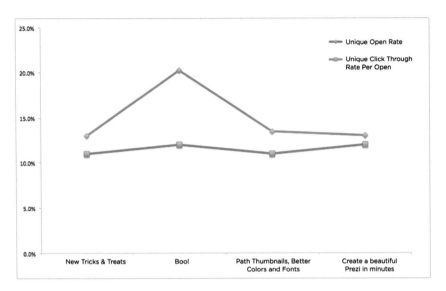

FIGURE 12.1   The open rates for the four Prezi email subject lines.

Source: Prezi

Malpass recalls his boss's response: "Why don't you try one that just says '*Boo!*'?" Malpass thought it was a terrible idea.

Malpass was planning to A/B test the subject line anyway, so he reluctantly threw "*Boo!*" into the mix and sent out emails with the four different subject lines to about a million users. He remembers the results with a smile: "*Boo!*" trounced the other three subject lines with a whopping 20 percent more opens (Figure 12.1).

Email also offers some intriguing opportunities for tests that don't have anything to do with either the content *or* the formatting. Namely, because email (unlike a website) *actively* reaches users (instead of passively awaiting their arrival), the *timing* of the message can itself be tested.

As it turns out, the *hour of the day* and the *day of the week* can both matter in a big way. Educational licenses make up a large portion of Prezi's user base, and Malpass was in for a surprise when he tested for the day of the week with the optimal open rate. He got

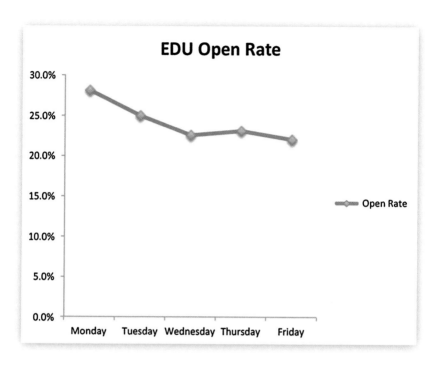

FIGURE 12.2   Open rate graph for educational licenses.

not one answer, but *two*: for educators, Monday had the highest open rate, and the rate decreased through the week (Figure 12.2). For non-educators, open rate peaked *late* in the week, on Thursday (Figure 12.3).

Price Testing

There's another pivotal element to every web business that's asking to be tested, beyond the layout and media and copy and even newsletter timing, and arguably even more important: the price. *Price testing* is a very valuable way to understand how demand for your product changes with price increases and decreases.

"Price testing is some of the most valuable testing and some of the most challenging technically," explains Scott Zakrajsek,

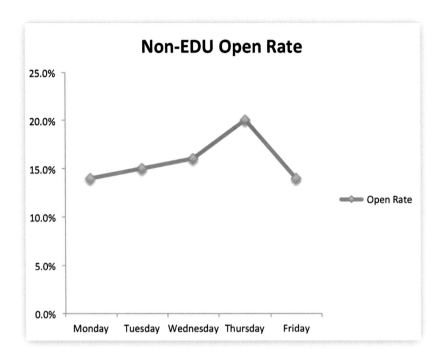

FIGURE 12.3   Open rate graph for non-educational licenses.

who has done testing at e-commerce sites like Adidas, Victoria's Secret, and Staples. "If you're a smaller site with ten to twenty key products, then price testing is the number-one thing you can do to maximize your conversion, your revenue."

The vast majority of prices today aren't really well thought through. It's easy to determine *cost-plus pricing*, where you take your own costs of production and add some kind of profit margin, as well as *competitive* or *market-based* pricing, but much trickier to come up with *value-based pricing*—getting the price in line with the value that you deliver.

With A/B testing, conventional wisdom and generalizations surrounding pricing become obsolete. There are many services out there where if you increase the price, just as many people will buy it. In some rare cases, and especially if your customers are buying something on behalf of their company, they are *more likely* to buy if the price is higher. Your customers might ask: if other businesses are paying this much for it, it must be good, right? Every product's and service's demand curve will look different, and *testing* prices is one of the best ways to get data about your own.

There's just as much theory and anecdote surrounding a price's trailing digits: the cents. Some people argue that round-dollar figures connote a premium product (and have design possibilities that include eliminating the decimal portion altogether); others argue that there is an important lure to prices that end in 99¢. Some authorities will argue the differences between 95¢, 96¢, 97¢, and 98¢; Walmart is known for its seemingly random cent-pricing ($6.37 toothpaste, $8.02 stapler), which seems to connote that prices have been cut to the bone. Where does that leave you and *your* business?

What's interesting is that these are all psychological tactics that are very difficult to understand fully or to generalize from another business's results to your own. By A/B testing them you can very quickly measure and see for yourself *exactly* how those factors are in play with your own business. You can plot your own price elasticity curve, and in some cases you'll see that if you increase the price, consumption stays the same. The only way to know for certain is to test it.

Testing the Perceived Price: The Last-Minute Discount

There are two hurdles to successful price testing. The first is technical: most prices are stored in a database or pricing table, and so any test that modifies the price of an item is going to need much *deeper technical integration* than a test simply involving only front-end design elements. The second hurdle is about managing customer relationships: to accidentally show users a lower price on the page and then charge them a higher price breaks not only customers' trust but the law. And users who are charged a higher price even if the site is transparent about it may feel betrayed or alienated when they learn that most other customers paid less.

There is a quick-and-easy method to foray into price testing that avoids *all* of these problems, something we call the *last-minute discount*. The way it works is quite simple. You show the customer a higher price (say $13.99) than the "actual" price of that item, which most users see (say $9.99) and which lives in the back-end price book. As the user in the $13.99 variation group moves down the checkout funnel, they discover *just before* confirming their purchase that a "last-minute discount" has been applied and that their total is in fact only $9.99! You've managed to get reasonably accurate information about what kind of conversion rate to expect from the higher price without dealing with back-end integration *or* worrying about making customers upset.

This type of cosmetic price testing is also perfect for testing the cents of a price. A product shown for $19.63, $19.95, and $19.99 in different tests could check out at $19.50 or $19.00 even; the users may not even notice the change. (Just be sure not to charge customers *more* than they're expecting!) Reading the conventional wisdom about cent pricing yields various—often mutually exclusive—theories and superstitions. The truth is that every business is different; you won't know until you test.

Anchoring in Action: Judy's Book Club

Another way to get data on your pricing without literally offering a product for different prices to different users is to test the way that product's price is *anchored*, or contextualized, for the customer. Consumers typically don't buy the most expensive options available, and many times they don't buy the least expensive, either. (Restaurants, for instance, will often mark up the *second-least-expensive* menu option.) Perhaps displaying only paid plans on your site will get users in at the lowest rung; perhaps offering a "Free" plan with virtually no features will help persuade users that adequate services can't be had for free. Try both.

Judy's Book is a "social search" tool and reviews website that caters to a family audience. Paid business listings are a primary way Judy's Book makes money: businesses get better search positioning and more robust profiles with photos if they pay a monthly fee. Judy's Book wanted to increase the number of businesses that sign up for paid listings, and General Manager Ali Alami hypothesized that positioning a column showing the few features included with a free listing alongside the many features included in the paid listings would increase signups for paid listings (Figure 12.4).

Showing a free listing column increased clicks on the signup button for the basic paid listing by 198.6 percent.

There are a number of additional anchoring techniques worth considering, and, of course, testing. For instance, try adding a tier *above* your most expensive tier in order to make the one beneath it seem less expensive. And try having a small price delta between the plan you *want* people to buy and the one just below it, with the goal being to get customers to think they're getting a bargain ("For just a *little* bit more, I get *all* this stuff!").

ORIGINAL   VARIATION

FIGURE 12.4 Two-column Judy's Book listing page versus three-column Judy's Book listing page.

Testing the Billing

You have options when it comes to how the price is broken down to the user as well. You might test representing the price as an annual subscription price or as a monthly cost. You might, for instance, have a monthly price prominently displayed but explain to the user that the product is in fact billed annually. (Just be sure it's clear how much customers will be billed so they don't get a surprise charge.) Testing will reveal how these differences affect conversion, average order value, churn, and so forth.

In testing their own pricing display, for instance, Prezi saw a 12.5 percent increase in signups from emphasizing the monthly breakdown of its annual cost (Figure 12.5).

It's worth keeping *localization effects* in mind here: there are markets like Brazil, for instance, where appliances and hardware are more typically bought with monthly payments than they are in countries like the United States. (Laws can also differ from country to country in ways that affect pricing.) Understanding your market will help you get your bearings, but as always, test and see what works best.

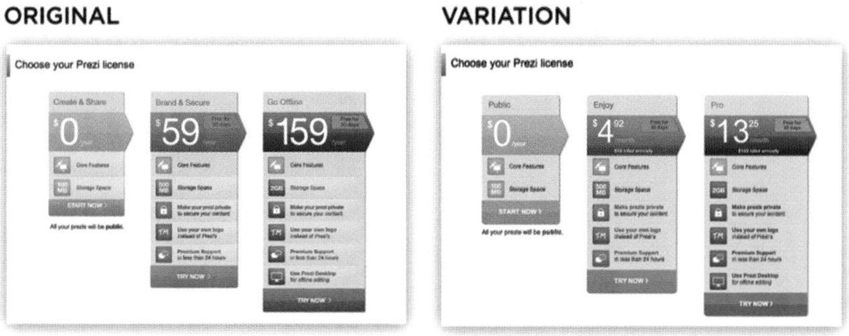

ORIGINAL   VARIATION

FIGURE 12.5   Prezi pricing displayed annually versus monthly.

Testing the Actual Price

Changing the *actual* price of a good or a service is the most complex of these approaches, in that it requires you to actually change your price book or to add additional SKUs. Full-fledged price testing has a world of nuances and best practices all its own. For instance, perhaps *serial testing* across *all* users at different *times* will avoid potential PR fallout rather than having different prices in play simultaneously. This method has its drawbacks, though: for instance, it becomes difficult to control for the general outside dynamics. One reason why you typically do A/B testing over *different* users in the *same* time period is to control for time-based effects, like day-of-week, time-of-day, news cycle, and the like. Typically, making meaningful sense of serialized price changes requires historical data that can put small-scale fluctuations into context.

A quick final reminder: it's absolutely critical when price testing to make sure you are *defining your success metrics* correctly. A higher price is very likely going to reduce conversions, but increase average order value: the key question is *by how much?* Make sure that you're using an appropriate metric, for instance, *revenue per visitor (RPV)*, which takes into account both conversion *and* average order value, in order to get accurate reporting from your testing tool about which variation is the winner. Consider, also, that even RPV may not tell the whole story. Higher pricing may lead to customer churn in the medium-term, so think carefully about what your results truly mean before making a major change.

TL;DR

- Not only the **subject lines** but the **timing** can be critical in influencing open rates and click-through rates for email. Roll out large email campaigns gradually, test variations, and then send the winner on to the rest of your list.

- **Price testing** can be one of the most important types of testing to conduct for your business, and there are a number of ways to do it.

- The **last-minute discount** is a great technique for testing price without needing to deal with back-end integration or worrying about upsetting users.

- **Anchoring** the price of a product into context with other prices can greatly affect how users react.

- **Presentation** can be everything when it comes to pricing. For a quick-and-easy price test, try various breakdowns (e.g., monthly, yearly, or weekly) and see what works best.

- **Serial testing** is one way to test prices without needing to show different users different prices at the same time; however, this advantage is offset by difficulties in ensuring the accuracy of its results.

13

Personalize, Personalize, Personalize

Moving Beyond the One-to-Many Web

Online retail giant Amazon has an army of engineers whose job it is to deliver an experience that maximizes profit per square inch for each page on the Amazon website. And they've realized that one of the best ways to do this is through personalization. They examine a user's entire history—the things someone has looked at, clicked on, or purchased—and then deliver exactly the thing they think is most valuable for *this* user.

Today's A/B testing tools offer advanced targeting and segmentation, allowing the non-Amazons of the world to create tailored experiences for different types of visitors. A business may start by using A/B testing to improve the "average best experience" on its website—a single experience across all types of users. The next step in the company's evolution of optimization is moving from honing the "average best experience" for everyone to grouping users into segments—and then using A/B testing to optimize the experience for each segment. A returning visitor could see a different interface than a new visitor; someone on a tablet could see something different from someone on a desktop; someone from Canada could see something different from someone from the United States. Each segment is an opportunity for optimization.

Targeting versus Segmentation

There are two things that Optimizely and other testing solutions enable to help sites make sense of their user populations: targeting and segmentation. *Targeting* happens *before the test* and is essentially the definition of who is allowed to see a particular experiment, based on the URL and any number of conditions. One cohort of visitors (say those who come to your site via social media) will see one variation while visitors coming from search engines will see a different one.

Segmentation happens *after the test* and takes a different approach: you run the experiment for everybody and then isolate different groups of segments *afterward* and figure out how each performed. A great example of where segmentation can be handy is with mobile and tablet browsers. Perhaps your proposed new page layout works great overall: you still want to make sure that it's not a *regression* or an inferior experience for users arriving on smartphones or tablets. For instance, perhaps a button element is too small to be comfortably clicked on a mobile screen: this would likely show up in a segmentation report, where the conversion and engagement of mobile users is lagging behind that of their desktop counterparts.

A growing number of websites are moving from providing one-to-many, average best experiences for all visitors to *one-to-few* experiences that involve smart targeting based on browser, location, behavior, and more. The final step in this evolution is the *one-to-one* web: a personal experience tailored for each individual user. It's easy to imagine that several years from now people will look back and be shocked at how generic, impersonal, and one-to-many the web we know today is. It's inevitable that the web will move toward a more personalized one-to-one experience and it's just a question of how that reality will come about. The vision for Optimizely is to enable businesses to show exactly the right thing to the right person at the right time. A/B testing is the first step toward this vision. Targeting and segmentation are the next step.

Using Segmentation to Drill Down into Test Results

Imagine that a company tries a new site layout and notices that overall sales increase. A slightly more detailed analysis might reveal that the sales decreased slightly for people who visited the site on tablet devices. The company then starts hypothesizing about why that happened and what was different for this visitor segment. The issue could be, for instance, that the new design pushed the "Add to Cart" button below the fold on an iPad and the user had to scroll down to tap it. That's a good hypothesis about what could be causing sales to drop, and a perfect place to begin a second experiment. The company targets a segment or audience (perhaps just iPad users) and tries to deliver an even better experience to them.

The natural testing cycle is usually to start off by examining the one-to-many results data: how did all website visitors react to the test? Then, slicing the data into granular pieces based on any number of conditions (UTM source, browser, cookies, referral URL, location) generates specific questions like, how did paid traffic react to the test? Results from specific segments in one experiment turn into the targeting criteria for the next experiment. Iterative loop closed!

Geo-Targeting, State by State: Romney 2012

From the start, the digital campaign team for Mitt Romney's 2012 presidential campaign considered increasing email signups on mittromney.com to be one of their primary goals. As Ryan Meerstein—a senior political analyst from Targeted Victory who ran testing and optimization for the Romney campaign—explains, "Email is still the golden goose of fundraising when you're making direct solicitations. We're seeing each email valued at anywhere between seven and eight dollars in future revenue."

Between May 2011 and November 2012, the Romney campaign's 140-person digital team along with Targeted Victory ran hundreds of tests. "Once we saw [how easy it was to conduct A/B testing], the ideas started flying. We wanted to start testing just about everything," Meerstein says. "We started on the splash page and when we saw success, we continued to build from there."

They tried showing different landing pages to visitors from different states, hypothesizing that visitors would sign up for email updates more if they saw a message specific to their state. They tested the state-specific geo-targeted message against a universal landing page lacking any state-specific messaging (Figure 13.1).

They found that when they simply added the state name (in the example in the figure, Florida) to the call to action text, visitors entered their email and zip code *19 percent more often*.

Starting in September 2012 and lasting until Election Day, visitors to mittromney.com received a distinct experience depending on their home state, which proved to be a valuable tool for the campaign. The data clearly showed that personalizing the message led to success. With this test as testament, the team decided to make the splash page specific for each state. They used geo-targeting to send visitors from each state to a page with a message specific to that state. They also crafted *personalized calls to action* based on absentee-vote states and early-vote states. Visitors from Ohio saw messages directing them to early voting locations; visitors from Colorado saw targeted messages for how to get an absentee ballot.

As a result, the Romney team saw not only greater signups on the splash page but more interaction with *local events* advertised on

FIGURE 13.1 Nationwide Romney 2012 email signup page versus state-specific Romney 2012 email signup page.

Source: Romney 2012.

the site, *especially* in the critical hours after voting started. "The thing that was great about it was that we could go [to our A/B testing tool] and set up the personalized experiences in thirty minutes," Meerstein says. "In the final weeks of the campaign, there's a huge difference between something being live on Tuesday morning and Thursday night."

When to Personalize and When *Not* to: Wikipedia

Wikipedia is a useful case study in the art of *not* tailoring the experience to every user. For instance, when Wikipedia's annual fundraising push comes around, the site is able to know that one user may be coming from Toronto for information about film directors, and another from Sydney for information about world history, but it shows both users (and *all* users) the very same message. That's a deliberate choice, and it also happens to be the *correct* one. How do they know this? They've tested it.

Through A/B testing, the fundraising team discovered that their users appear to be *less* likely to donate when faced with a targeted fundraising appeal than with a universal one. It could be that users find personalization intrusive, or it could be that part of Wikipedia's brand is its openness and universality.

The Wikipedia example illustrates that despite its incredible power as a tool, personalization isn't *always* going to be more effective. Sometimes the "average best" is in fact simply "best." The web is not a place for static universal truths, and personalization is no exception. How is a company to know whether personalization will take its success metrics to the next level, or set them back? There is only one answer: *test it.*

TL;DR

- **Segmentation** allows you to compare how different segments of users responded to the same experience. Differences that you observe between groups can be illuminating and give you an opportunity to go beyond the **average best experience** of the one-to-many web toward an improved one-to-few experience.
- **Targeting** is deliberately providing different types of users with different experiences, and can be a powerful technique under many circumstances.
- Consider how your user experience may or may not be optimized across different **platforms**, screen dimensions, touch input versus mouse input, and so on.
- Sometimes **geo-targeting**, or tailoring users' experience based on their location, can be an extremely powerful way to optimize beyond the "average best."
- While personalization is frequently a boon for your success metrics, occasionally a **universal** call to action works better than a targeted one. Test to make sure personalization is working for your key success metrics.

Conclusion

In this book we've tried to demonstrate the power of what A/B testing can bring to your own organization. We've seen examples from companies and teams across a number of fields: what they tried, what they learned, and how a few simple questions turned into a cultural sea change.

We've explored some of the most important overarching principles for A/B testing. We showed the importance of defining quantifiable success metrics, and why you should seek the global maximum. By looking at case studies, we uncovered the idea that sometimes less is more, and that words matter. Not every single test, of course, will be an instant success, which is why it's important to fail fast and learn. And we hope we've persuaded you that the best time to start is today.

We've laid out a roadmap that starts by choosing a testing solution that's right for you. In month one you should identify your first experiment and get buy-in from your company's stakeholders and decision makers. The evolution continues in months two to five as you build a testing culture, a team, and a process within your organization. And from month six and beyond, we've outlined some of the components of building out a long-term strategy that includes testing as an ongoing iterative process that is wedded not only to evaluation but to creativity and design as well.

We've also explored some advanced topics in A/B testing, such as potential cautions and hazards you may encounter along the way, how to take testing beyond page elements, and how to go beyond the "average best" experience and into targeting, segmentation, and personalization.

We hope you feel inspired to ask questions, to test possible solutions, and to evangelize—to become an internal advocate for testing in your own organization.

The methods and approaches we discuss in this book are all part of a bigger story and a longer journey of helping your company and the world at large to become more data-driven. There is a broader cultural shift from the top-down management style of old to the analytical, quantitative, measurable, data-driven style of the future.

A/B testing is at the vanguard of this massive shift. Now not only can you come up with creative, interesting ways to improve a user's experience—you can measure that. Since for the first time it is now possible to clearly measure what works and what doesn't work, businesses will evolve to focus on trying to ask the right questions and not prescribing the "right" answers.

And the right questions can change everything.

60 Things to A/B Test

Always be testing, and you'll always be measuring ways to improve your conversion rates and business. The more you test, the more you understand about how your website visitors respond and behave. The hardest part of A/B testing is determining what to test in the first place. After having worked with thousands of customers who do A/B testing every day, one of the most common questions we still hear is, "Where do I begin?"

Website testing inherently generates more questions than it answers, so your first test can lead to a whole litany of follow-up tests. If you treat each test as a part of a continuous cycle of testing and learning, like the cycle in Figure A-1.1, then follow-up tests (and higher conversions) will come naturally.

Here are 60 ideas for things to test on your website today to get you started.

Calls to Action

Your website exists for visitors to take action: reading, purchasing, signing up, downloading, or sharing. Here are some ways to test calls to action that can yield quick, easy, and big wins.

1. *Buy now? Purchase? Check out? Add to cart?* Change the call to action (CTA) text on your buttons to see which word or phrase converts more visitors.
2. Try varying the location of your CTA button, making some CTAs more prominent than others.

FIGURE A-1.1 The iterative testing loop.

3. Test multiple CTAs per page against one CTA per page.

4. Change buttons to hyperlinks to find out which display your users prefer.

5. Find out if CTAs with text, icons, or text plus icons convert more users on your site.

6. Test different colors, shapes, and sizes for CTA buttons on your website.

Content

Content fuels your online business, particularly if you're a B2B company. Testing how you position and advertise content on your site can uncover big conversion and engagement lifts.

7. Test gated content against nongated content. Find out if your users are willing to sign up or provide more information to access materials on your site.

8. Do site visitors crave more information about your company before signing up or making a purchase? Test adding or removing "About" content on your home page.

9. Content tone can make a big difference in keeping users on your site. See what your visitors prefer by testing various tones and styles.

10. Test how your content is displayed. Do users prefer to scroll down the page or click through to another page to learn more?

Copy

Copy is your direct line of communication with website visitors— it sets the tone and helps users understand what you're all about. Use these tests to make the copy on your site better resonate with your audience.

11. Test different headline texts. Try variations that are straight-forward against ones that are abstract, goofy, or creative.

12. Find out if your site visitors prefer shorter versions of head-lines, taglines, product descriptions, and other content on your site.

13. Run a multivariate test. Test different combinations of head-lines and taglines in combination with the visual imagery on your page to find the ultimate winning variation.

14. Test paragraphs versus bulleted lists.

15. Test how you frame your copy. Users may have different reactions to positive versus negative messaging.

16. Try making your site easier to read with larger fonts, higher-contrast colors, and professional fonts (not Comic Sans). Studies show this increases trustworthiness and increases conversions.

Visual Media

Digital media have the power to greatly influence conversions and engagement on a website, and testing digital media is a great idea because the right media can subconsciously influence people to act in a way that's aligned with your testing goals.

17. Test different types of images on your landing page. People versus products is a good place to start.
18. And iterate from there! Try a static image versus a product video versus a 360° product image.
19. See how a stock image stacks up against an image of your employees or customers in action.
20. Test a rotating carousel on your home page versus a static image or video.
21. Test different voice-overs for the videos on your site. Test whether a male or a female voice leads to the most completed views.
22. Try different variations of your site's product demo: animated versus screencast.
23. Test auto-play against click-to-play video.

Funnels

If your goal is to get more people from one page to the next—like in a checkout funnel, signup flow, or lead nurture—then A/B testing is your best bet. Funnels are rife with low-hanging fruit to test.

24. Test removing extraneous distractions—like product offers, promotions, or shipping information—from each page in the purchase flow. Oftentimes a simplified experience can drive more conversions.

25. Test the number of pages in your funnel. How does packing more information on one page compare to spreading information across multiple pages?

26. Test removing navigation to any pages outside the checkout funnel.

27. Or try replacing certain steps within your funnel with modal boxes. For example, try making shipping options a modal box instead of a page.

Site Navigation

From the moment a visitor lands on your site, the navigation menu sets a foundation—it's how people maneuver your site's flow and prioritize what's important. Here are some ideas for how to make it better:

28. Test the order of menu items in your site navigation.

29. Test the display of your navigation bar. Do site visitors prefer a horizontal or vertical orientation?

30. Or what about a fixed navigation bar that travels down the page as your site visitors scroll?

31. Test out the title of your navigation items. A simple change, like "Why Use Us" to "How It Works," may have a significant impact.

32. *Testing Tip:* If a test fails, try targeting the test to new versus returning visitors. Returning visitors are accustomed

to seeing the site in a certain way—if a link or menu item is missing from the spot they normally go to in order to find it, they're not going to do the work to locate it.

Forms

Any potential friction point on a website is prime for testing. Forms are frequently cumbersome areas of websites. Try these tests on the forms on your site:

33. Test the length of signup forms. Try removing nonessential signup boxes or relocating them to a page further down the funnel.

34. Try a special offer, discount, or promotion to increase sign-ups. People love free stuff.

35. Spam is the worst. Try adding text that assures users you won't fill up their inboxes with unnecessary junk.

36. Try making individual form fields larger. Larger fields feel more friendly.

37. Try asking for different information in your form fields—for example, business email versus regular email, or work phone versus mobile phone.

Mobile Site

The mobile web is pervasive. Improving your mobile website through testing will help create an optimized experience that generates more click-throughs, revenue, and conversions.

38. Test the length of your mobile web pages. Are mobile users more willing to click to a new page or scroll down a page when browsing your site on their devices?

39. Try different displays and navigation options. Blinds, buttons, and blocks are good places to start.

Testing Tip: When testing your mobile website, try targeting mobile users based on their operating system—Android or iOS, for example—to learn more about your mobile website visitors.

Advertising

A/B testing increases the value of the money you're already spending on marketing programs, such as search engine marketing. To ensure you're getting the biggest bang for your buck out of each paid initiative, try these tests:

40. Test the headlines on your paid campaigns to see which ones get the most clicks.
41. Try changing up the display URL on your ads. This can impact how many visitors click the ad.
42. The landing page each ad directs to is an excellent place for testing. You paid for that visitor to land there, so you want to do everything you can to convert that visitor.

Social

The reasons someone would share your site are many—make it easy for them to do so. Here are a few tests to increase likes, retweets, and +1s on your content:

43. Change the size and placement of social icons to see what compels users to share more often.
44. Test standard social media icons against ones you've designed to match the look and feel of your site.

45. Try finding your optimal Twitter voice. Tweet the same link with different types of text at the same time two days in a row and see which tone of voice gets more engagement.

46. Test different types of customer reviews on your site to see which are most compelling to your audience. Some examples include testimonials, Yelp reviews, and ResellerRatings.

Email

How do you make sure your marketing emails get opened and, dare we say, clicked? Here are some testable elements that can increase open rates and click-throughs:

47. Test length and copy of your email subject lines.

48. Test personalized versus unpersonalized emails by using the recipient's name in the subject or email text.

49. Find the optimal time to reach your audience by measuring open rates on different days of the week and at different times of the day.

50. If you distribute a newsletter or email update, see how a weekly send stacks up against a monthly blast.

51. Would readers prefer an email from your CEO, your marketing director, your broader team, or someone else? Test different "from" addresses to find out.

Personalize It

Today, we're more accustomed to web experiences that are custom-tailored to who we are and the URLs we've come from. Try testing these personalization techniques and see if visitors convert better.

52. Create seasonal or holiday-specific promotional offers and test them on visitors living in specific locations.

53. Test auto-filling form fields related to a site visitor's location. Make things easier for your users.

54. Test matching language-specific content to users coming from a certain country or region.

55. Test different page designs and messaging for new versus returning visitors.

56. Test whether showing different landing pages for visitors coming from mobile devices versus desktop browsers performs better than having the same landing page for both.

Pricing and Shipping

Finding the right pricing point can drive more visitors to make a purchase. Use these tests to maximize revenue from your site:

57. Test offering a free trial versus a money-back guarantee to see which converts more users in the short term and in the long term.

58. Test having checkboxes auto-selected as default (such as billing information being the same as shipping info).

59. On your pricing page, test whether annual billing or monthly billing generates more subscriptions.

60. Try anchoring customers high before showing them a lower price. For example, "Competitors charge $2.9 trillion, but you can use us for just $2.99!"

Metrics and the Statistics behind A/B Testing

By Bryan Gumm

As online marketers and product managers, we can choose to optimize our users' experience along several different metrics. For example, a product manager of a subscription service might be interested in optimizing retention rate (percent), and an online marketer of an e-commerce site might focus on optimizing average order value ($). While each of these is obviously valid, the statistics behind A/B testing are slightly different for each. Before delving into the nuances of each, we'll introduce a few core concepts.

Confidence Intervals

Suppose we know that 51.4 percent of the population of the City of San Francisco has a bachelor's degree or higher. If we were to choose 1,000 city residents at random, we'd expect that exactly 514 of those people would have a bachelor's degree or higher. In reality, of course, this rarely happens. Why not? First, depending on your sample size, it may not be mathematically possible to arrive at exactly 51.4 percent (try this example with a sample size of 100 instead of 1,000). Second (and more important), by using a small sample to represent a large population, we are introducing some error.

In reality, it's usually difficult or impossible to measure the *exact* value of a statistic for an entire population; hence the obvious value of sampling. It seems, then, that we need a way to quantify the reliability of our sample data. We do this using estimates.

When we talk about statistics from a sample, we tend to provide two types of estimates: point estimates (single numbers) and interval estimates (two numbers). If we were to poll 1,000 city residents chosen randomly, and found that 509 respondents had earned a bachelor's degree or higher, our point estimate would be 50.9 percent (509/1,000). The interval estimate is slightly more complex and depends partly on how certain we need to be in our estimate. The latter, often called the desired confidence level, varies by application, but for most A/B testing and other business analytics in general, 95 percent confidence is the standard. In the next section, we'll dive more into confidence levels.

For the time being, let's assume a 95 percent desired confidence level. The formula for the 95 percent interval estimate is given by:

$$\hat{p} \pm 1.96\sqrt{\frac{\hat{p}(1-\hat{p})}{n}} \tag{E.1}$$

where:

$\hat{p} =$ Our point estimate (50.9% or 0.509)

$1.96 =$ A normal curve Z-value estimate corresponding to 95% significance

$n =$ Our sample size (1,000)

For our example, the interval estimate would be:

$$\hat{p} \pm 1.96\sqrt{\frac{\hat{p}(1-\hat{p})}{n}}$$

$$0.509 \pm 1.96\sqrt{\frac{0.509(1-0.509)}{1,000}}$$

$$0.509 \pm 0.031$$

We interpret that by saying we are 95 percent confident that the rate of San Francisco residents having a bachelor's degree or better is between 47.8 and 54.0 percent.

If we are instead interested in the average age of a San Francisco resident, the approach is the same and the formula very similar.

$$\bar{x} \pm 1.96\sqrt{\frac{s^2}{n}} \tag{E.2}$$

where:

$\bar{x}$ = The average age from our sample

n = Our sample size

s^2 = The variance in age from our sample

The sample variance calculation is given by:

$$s^2 \frac{\sum_{i=1}^{n} (x_i - \bar{x})^2}{n - 1} \tag{E.3}$$

This formula says:

x_i Take the age value for each resident.

$x_i - \bar{x}$ Subtract from that value the average age of the sample.

$(x_i - \bar{x})^2$ Square the result.

$\sum_{i=1}^{n} (x_i - \bar{x})^2$ Sum all of those values together.

$\frac{\sum_{i=1}^{n} (x_i - \bar{x})^2}{n - 1}$ Divide by the sample size less 1.

If your data is in Excel, you can compute the sample mean and variance by using the average( ) and var( ) formulas, respectively.

The curious reader might ask why the confidence interval formula used when measuring an average is different from the formula used when measuring a percentage. In fact, they're exactly the same! To see this for yourself, try simplifying the variance term (s^2) when every data point (x_i) is known to be either 1 or 0, which is the case when measuring a percentage. (Hint: When x_i is either 1 or 0, note that $x_i^2 = x_i$.)

For both the average age and the percentage of degree holders measurements, there are three conditions that result in a large confidence interval:

1. High variance in our data (inconsistent data).
2. A small sample (not enough data points).
3. A high desired confidence (greater than 95 percent).

In other words, to reduce the size of the interval, we'll need to take a larger sample, select a metric with less variability, or accept lower confidence in our results.

A percentage measurement has a unique property that its variance depends only on the percentage value itself:

$$s_{\hat{p}}^2 = \hat{p}(1 - \hat{p}) \qquad\qquad (E.4)$$

If we plot this function (Figure A-2.1), we can easily see that the variance of a percentage measurement is maximized when the point estimate is 0.5.

Therefore, it is possible to reduce variance (and reduce overall required sample size) if a metric whose expected value is closer to 0 or 1 is selected.

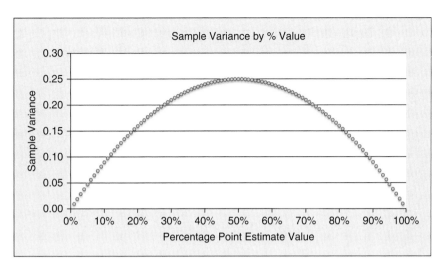

FIGURE A-2.1 Sample variance by percentage point estimate value.

Confidence Levels

As mentioned earlier, the standard confidence level for most business applications is 95 percent. Other than its pervasiveness, there is no reason statistical studies need to be limited to 95 percent. In other applications, such as biomedical research, manufacturing, or statistical computing, it is not uncommon to use other confidence levels (80 percent, 90 percent, and 99 percent are other common ones).

So what does a confidence level actually mean, anyway? Recall that earlier we said a 95 percent confidence level indicates we are 95 percent confident the true population value lies between 47.8 percent and 54.0 percent. In that example, we happened to know the true value was 51.4 percent, so our interval was correct. What a 95 percent confidence level actually tells us is that if we repeated the survey many, many times and computed a confidence interval for each, 95 percent of those confidence intervals would

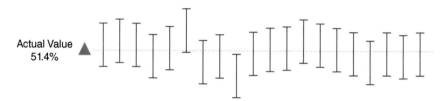

Actual Value
51.4%

FIGURE A-2.2   Confidence intervals per sample.

contain the true population value. In the case depicted in Figure A-2.2, one of the 20 samples did not contain the true value of 51.4 percent.

In practice, we don't take multiple samples; we take one or two. For that reason, it becomes important to select the right metric and ensure that the sample size is sufficiently large to detect differences in the key performance indicator (KPI) of interest.

Recall from formula E.1 we said the value 1.96 corresponded to a 95 percent confidence interval. You can obtain this value for any confidence interval you want using the Excel functions found in Table A-2.1.

TABLE A-2.1   Excel Functions for Confidence Levels

Confidence Level	Excel Formula	Approximate Value
80%	=NORMSINV(0.90)	1.28
90%	=NORMSINV(0.95)	1.65
95%	=NORMSINV(0.975)	1.96
99%	=NORMSINV(0.995)	2.58

To determine what number to pass the NORMSINV function, first let your desired confidence level be represented by $(1 - \alpha)$. Then if b is the number passed to Excel, we find b by the following function:

$$b = 1 - \frac{\alpha}{2}$$

(E.5)

For example, for the 95 percent confidence level, compute:

$$(1 - \alpha) = 0.95$$
$$\alpha = 0.05$$
$$b = 1 - \frac{0.05}{2} = 0.975$$

With the confidence interval foundation laid, we can now better explain how A/B test statistics work.

A/B Testing Metrics Framework

The preceding examples all dealt with a single sample. In A/B testing, however, we are interested in comparing multiple samples. For purposes of simplicity, here we will focus on two-sample comparisons (a simple A/B paradigm).

Suppose we wanted to compare conversion for two variants: current versus test. Using the principles applied earlier, we could derive point and interval estimates for each of the two versions. If we plot those side by side (Figure A-2.3), we then get a sense of how different the two experiences are in terms of that metric.

In the first case, we can visually see that versions A and B are not very different from one another. Case 2 shows a little more distinction between the two versions, and Case 3 shows the most differentiation between the two versions.

While visual inspection is always helpful, we need some way to empirically say whether A and B are "different enough." That is, we need a concrete formula to tell us when the observed difference between two observed conversion rates in an A/B test is large enough that it can reasonably be attributed to the difference in experience between A and B, and not just to a sampling error.

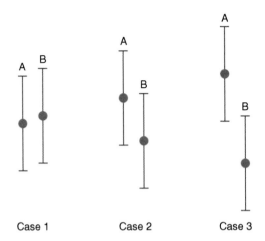

FIGURE A-2.3 Conversion comparisons for two variants.

There is an entire field of statistics devoted to defining "different enough" in multisample comparisons. That field is experimental design, a field in which there exist dozens of great books and an abundance of academic research (starting in the early 1900s). In most cases, we use the data we have to produce a test statistic. If that test statistic gets far enough away from 0, we conclude that the observed differences are likely not due to random chance. We will explore two such statistics.

The Z Statistic for Two Proportions

If our metric is a percentage or a proportion, the test statistic is given by:

$$Z = \frac{\hat{p}_B - \hat{p}_A}{\sqrt{p(1-p)\left(\dfrac{1}{n_B} + \dfrac{1}{n_A}\right)}} \qquad \text{(E.6)}$$

From an earlier section, the denominator should look familiar to you. In its most basic form, it can be thought of as a measure of the overall variation in the metric we are examining (called the standard error). In fact, most basic test statistics follow this same general form:

$$Test\ Statistic = \frac{Observed\ Differences}{Standard\ Error} \qquad (E.7)$$

For two proportions, the standard error is obtained by combining all values (irrespective of original group), computing the combined proportion, and then normalizing by the two sample sizes. If X_A is the number of people who converted in the first sample and X_B is that for the second, the combined conversion rate is given by:

$$p = \frac{X_B + X_A}{n_B + n_A} \qquad (E.8)$$

For a computational example, suppose we have:

$$
\begin{aligned}
n_B &= 49{,}981 \quad n_A = 50{,}332 \\
X_B &= 42{,}551 \quad X_A = 42{,}480 \\
\hat{p}_B &= 0.851 \quad \hat{p}_A = 0.844
\end{aligned}
$$

We first compute p.

$$
\begin{aligned}
p &= \frac{42{,}511 + 42{,}480}{49{,}981 + 50{,}332} \\
p &= \frac{85{,}031}{100{,}313} \\
p &= 0.8477
\end{aligned}
$$

We then compute our test statistic.

$$Z = \dfrac{0.851 - 0.844}{\sqrt{0.8477(1 - 0.8477)\left(\dfrac{1}{50,332} + \dfrac{1}{49,981}\right)}}$$

$$Z = 3.09$$

Note that if you were following along on your own, you may have ended up with a Z-value of 3.24. The difference is due to rounding.

Based on this test statistic, we can compute the probability that our observed difference (-0.007) is due to random chance. This value, called the p-value, is the area underneath the standard normal (Z) distribution before or after a certain point. If the value of Z is negative, we compute the value *up to* that point, and multiply it by 2. If the value of Z is positive, we compute the value *after* that point, and then multiply it by 2. The multiplication by 2 is the application of what is called a two-tailed test, which will be clarified later.

In Excel, it is simple to produce the two-tailed p-value using this formula: NORMSDIST(-ABS(Z))*2. For our value of 3.09, this results in a p-value of 0.0021. This means that there is only a 0.2 percent chance that the difference we observed is due to random chance. If not due to random chance, it must be due to the differential experience. Put another way, there is a 99.8 percent chance that version B increases conversion above version A. This is the number many statistical packages, including Optimizely, publish as the "chance to beat original" metric (though Optimizely uses a one-tailed test).

The difference between a one- and two-tailed p-value is that in the latter, we are curious to know whether the two metrics differ at all, whereas in the former, we care only if one metric is greater than the other. The latter is often the case in A/B testing. Institutional learning aside, having a current version (A) that outperforms a new version (B) isn't very actionable, but if we find a new version (B) that outperforms the existing version (A), we will likely take action and make the new version become the default. For that reason, many online marketers and product managers use one-tailed tests.

If conducting a one-tailed test, it is important to order the numerator of the Z statistic such that the new version's metric is first, as is the case in formula E.6. This becomes important in the computation of the "chance to beat original" estimate. For a properly formed one-tailed test, the p-value can be obtained in Excel using the formula 1-NORMSDIST(Z). The "chance to beat original" is simply NORMSDIST(Z).

Why is the order of the metrics in the numerator important? If we applied formula E.9 instead, our statistic would be -3.09. If that value is plugged in to the Excel functions above, the p-value and "chance to beat original" would be reversed.

$$Z = \frac{\hat{p}_A + \hat{p}_B}{\sqrt{p(1-p)\left(\dfrac{1}{n_B} + \dfrac{1}{n_A}\right)}} \tag{E.9}$$

The Z test for proportions is acceptable to use as long as the sample size is sufficiently large and random sampling is applied. Common test statistics books call for a sample size of at least 30 to 50 in each group being compared, but in the A/B testing space, we often greatly exceed this.

The *t* Statistic for Two Averages

If our metric of interest is an average instead of a proportion, the basic concepts are the same, though there are more assumptions, legwork, and input to do these tests properly.

The basic *t* statistic is given by

$$t = \frac{\bar{x}_B - \bar{x}_A}{s_p \sqrt{\dfrac{1}{n_B} + \dfrac{1}{n_A}}} \qquad\qquad \text{(E.10)}$$

where:

$\bar{x}_B =$ The sample average for experience B

$n_B =$ The sample size for experience B

$s_p =$ The combined sample standard deviation for both experiences

The combined sample standard deviation is given by:

$$s_p = \sqrt{\frac{(n_B - 1)s_B^2 + (n_A - 1)s_A^2}{n_B + n_A - 2}} \qquad\qquad \text{(E.11)}$$

The sample variance formulas were given earlier.

Finally, because we are interested in the difference between two averages but must compute two standard deviate ons in order to arrive at a decision, we must account for that secondary estimation by incorporating a concept known as degrees of freedom. For this *t* test, the degrees of freedom are given by:

$$df = n_B + n_A - 2 \qquad\qquad \text{(E.12)}$$

The "2" in formula E.12 represents the number of other parameters we must estimate.

In Excel, the formula to compute the p-value is TDIST(ABS (t),df,tails) where tails is 1 or 2 depending on the type of p-value we want. As was the case with the p-value in the last section, the "chance to beat original" is 1 minus the p-value. Again, if we are employing a one-tailed test, the order in which the terms appear in the numerator of the t statistic is important.

There are far more assumptions involved in using this test than there were for the Z test for proportions.

Random sampling is used to determine who gets experience A versus B.

The two population variances are equal.

The sample sizes are sufficiently large (>50 or so for each experience).

The underlying populations are approximately normally distributed (i.e., they follow a bell curve).

When statisticians talk about the assumptions of a test, they are referring to the original assumptions under which the test statistic was developed. It is often the case that those assumptions are made, the test statistic is developed, and then those assumptions are challenged. In the latter stage, the statistician will purposely violate the assumptions and analytically determine what happens to the overall measure. If the statistician finds that the overall test statistic is still valid, then the statistic is said to be robust to that assumption (i.e., it can be relaxed).

There is a lot of published research on what to do when assumptions aren't met. If you are concerned with this, further reading can be found in the Wikipedia article "Student's t-test" with some referencing links on that site.

Acknowledgments

This book would not have happened if it were not for the heroic efforts of our phenomenal team, in particular, Cara Harshman and Brian Christian.

It was during a late-afternoon meeting not too long ago when we first asked Cara to help us take on the challenge of writing this book. It was clear to her how big of an opportunity it was to help tell this story and she left that first meeting with unbridled enthusiasm. After dozens of interviews, countless hours of hard work, and many late nights that enthusiasm has not waned. Thank you, Cara.

Brian Christian's original article in *Wired*[1] about A/B testing inspired us to write this book. He was one of the first to write about how A/B testing has led to a cultural transformation away from the HiPPO syndrome toward a meritocracy of ideas and data-driven decision making. It has been a real privilege to have had Brian's help writing this book.

We'd also like to thank the team at John Wiley & Sons, including Richard Narramore, Lydia Dimitriadis, Christine Moore, and Deborah Schindlar. Their support and guidance along the way have been essential to the success of this project.

---

[1] "The A/B Test: Inside the Technology That's Changing the Rules of Business," *Wired*, May 2012.

The feedback from everyone who read early manuscripts of this book has also been tremendously helpful. In particular, we'd like to thank Brooks Bell, Caleb Whitmore, Chris Neumann, Hannah Harrison, Jon Miller, Marianne Siroker, and Teresa Harrison.

The real heroes in this book are the marketers in the trenches who do the hard work of helping transform their organization into a data-driven one. We were lucky enough to interview many of these heroes and we'd like to thank them: Bryan Gumm of Netflix, Dan McKinley of Etsy, David Harris of CareerBuilder, David Malpass of Prezi, Ed Wu of Dell, Eric Dorf of Lumosity, Eric Ries of The Lean Startup, Jarred Colli of Rocket Lawyer, Jeff Blettner of Formstack, Keval Desai of Digg, Kyle Duford of Chrome Industries, Kyle Rush of Obama for America, Lizzie Allen of IGN, Nazli Yuzak of Dell, Richard White of UserVoice, Ryan Meerstein of Targeted Victory, Scott Zakrajsek of Adidas, Steve Mardenfeld of Etsy, and Zack Exley of Wikimedia.

We would not have been able to write this book without the tremendous work of the entire team at Optimizely. We are the luckiest guys in the world to be able to work with such an incredible group of people every day. Thank you, all.

And last but certainly not least we'd like to thank our families. Their unconditional love and support have allowed us to pursue our passions in life. This book is dedicated to them.

Index